Modern Painting in Canada

Terry Fenton & Karen Wilkin

Modern Painting in Canada

Major Movements in Twentieth Century Canadian Art

Hurtig Publishers
in co-operation with The Edmonton Art Gallery

This book is based upon a catalogue and exhibition
produced by The Edmonton Art Gallery which were made
possible with the generous support of the Canada Council,
the Museum Assistance Programmes of the National Museums
of Canada Corporation, the Commonwealth Games Foundation
and Canadian Pacific. The show "Modern Painting
in Canada" was exhibited at The Edmonton Art Gallery
from July 7 to August 30, 1978.

Hurtig Publishers
10560 105 Street
Edmonton, Alberta
T5H 2W7

Canadian Cataloguing in Publication Data

Fenton, Terry.
    Modern painting in Canada

    ISBN 0-88830-162-6

    1. Painting, Canadian.   2. Painting,
Modern — 20th century — Canada.   3. Painters —
Canada — Biography.   I. Wilkin, Karen.
II. Title.
ND245.F45   759.11   C78-002110-X

Printed and bound in Canada

Contents

Introduction

The following essays by Karen Wilkin and myself do not purport to be a new history of Canadian painting in this century so much as a series of reflections prompted by the existing histories and our own experiences of Canadian art. It isn't a comprehensive survey. For one thing, we chose to concentrate on the major movements and groups of painters which were influential in Canada during this period, particularly the ones which were instrumental, in some way, in establishing modern — or modernist — painting in this country. Of necessity, we had to omit some deserving artists. For that, we apologize. Space limitations, as much as our theme, itself, made it impossible to be as comprehensive and inclusive as we would have wished.

Modern painting in Canada developed hand in hand with Canadian nationalism. From the outset, it was an uneasy partnership, characterized by misunderstandings, public quarrels, and outright struggles for ascendence. Because this continuing quarrel lies at the heart of Canada's search for her elusive identity, we are convinced that its history needs to be re-examined.

Terry Fenton

Canadians . . . are not as historically minded as the English, and, unlike the Americans . . . have not been brought up in a thorough knowledge of their own history. They cling to old myths, and are easily sold new and spurious inventions.[1]

Donald Creighton

The Group of Seven

The success of the Group of Seven and the legend of its lost leader, Tom Thomson, is the central fact in the history of Canadian art in this century. The rapidity, extent and duration of that success was phenomenal. Although Thomson painted seriously for only six years prior to his death in 1917, he had paintings purchased by The National Gallery of Canada during that brief career.[2] The Group of Seven wasn't formally created until 1920. From the beginning it was supported by The National Gallery as well as by influential public and private collectors. When the Royal Canadian Academy objected to The National Gallery's appointment to select Canadian paintings for the British Empire Exhibition at Wembley in 1924 (presumably because of the Gallery's acknowledged bias towards the Group), the Group and the Gallery defended themselves and triumphed. The Group of Seven emerged from the controversy as the "official" Canadian art establishment. Thereafter, it dictated taste in Canada until well into the 1940s, more than a decade after its official dissolution.

But, despite the achievement of Thomson and other members of the Group, the claims made for their art were — and continue to be — exaggerated. A myth surrounds their art which has inhibited subsequent development and which, ironically, distorts the recognition of their own achievements.

This myth maintains that Thomson was an uncommonly inspired, "natural" artist and that he invented a new, entirely Canadian manner — virtually uninfluenced by Europe — from his experience of the Canadian North. It was perpetuated by the Group of Seven and its supporters, especially A. Y. Jackson, who believed that only a Thomson-like transformation of the Canadian landscape could forge an original, national art.

It was perpetuated with the cooperation of the Ontario cultural establishment and English Canada generally. In its proclamation of a kind of experience which seemed uniquely Canadian, the art of the Group of Seven proposed to unite a recently-organized, naturally-divided country which sprawled, empire-like, from coast to coast across North America. It became the first, and strongest, nationalist art the country had known. And, in achieving this, it brought modern art to Canada.

Canada is a tenuous nation. In 1867, confederation established a territorial dominion based on a federation of provinces from three distinct areas in British North America: Ontario, Quebec and the Maritimes. This federation obtained rights to a huge block of potentially colonial territory stretching above the 49th parallel west to the Pacific and north to the Arctic Ocean. Parts of this western territory were in immediate danger of being annexed by the United States which, upon its recovery from the Civil War, was rapidly expanding westward. To claim this territory for Canada, the united provinces had to occupy it. But occupation meant financing a railroad to and through it. Because an enterprise of that magnitude couldn't be undertaken by any one province, it can be argued that the nation was created to finance a railroad.

The province of Ontario stood to benefit most from the economic and political consequences of confederation.

An intercontinental railroad would provide it with year-round access to the Maritime seaports as well as immediate access to the undeveloped West. But a great barrier — the Canadian Shield — stood between it and the fertile, agricultural land of the western prairies. This inhospitable wilderness of Precambrian rock, lake and bush stretched for a thousand miles across what is now western Ontario and eastern Manitoba, splitting the country in two. Although the Shield had traditionally provided Ontario with raw materials, mainly fur and lumber, it wasn't suited to agriculture and could be only sparsely settled.

Tom Thomson and the Group of Seven — an Ontario-based group of painters — seized upon this "Northland" and made it stand for Canada, much as the frontier (in this century, the Wild West of the movies) stands for the United States. Significantly, they discovered an archetypical Canadian landscape in the chief barrier to western expansion. They didn't seek it (let alone find it) in the West.

Apart from a few artists who had been patronized by the CPR and C. W. Jefferys, who made several trips to Saskatchewan and Alberta in the early 20th century, painters had seldom worked in the West and none had captured the national imagination. The North was more central to Canadian experience. Settlement in central Canada had traditionally been limited to small, fertile — or marginally fertile — areas surrounded by wilderness. The North was omnipresent.

But there was another reason. Like the United States during the 19th century, Canada had to establish a unique, cultural identity — above all, one that was non-European. And, again like the United States, it turned to painting for images of it.

During the 19th century in Europe, nationalist sentiments were seldom embodied in painting.[3] They were more commonly associated with music — perhaps because European nations had extensive "peasant" musical traditions which could be identified with national cultures. In frontier societies like the great North American nation states, folk traditions were either European or aboriginal. As the great age of nation building was also the great age of migration to the New World, both Canada and the United States became culturally diversified at the very time nationalism became vitally important to them. Because they lacked a common "people", they turned to their vast territories for images of unity. In each country (although

at different times), the land, and depictions of it, were called upon to awaken nationalist sentiments. "With respect to landscapes," said Henry David Thoreau, "I am monarch of all I *survey...*" Or, as folk singers put it nowadays, "this land belongs to you and me."

In the 19th century, painters of the Hudson River School in the United States sought what William Cullen Bryant called "that wilder image". The phrase, taken from a poem Bryant addressed to the painter, Thomas Cole, referred to a New World landscape which was untamed and non-European. However, if the landscape they depicted wasn't European, the tradition they worked within was. The conventions which governed their art had been developed during the 17th and 18th centuries in Europe and were formulated, in the 19th, by the English critic, John Ruskin. They sought to convey sublimity by depicting cataclysmic, awesome scenery, frequently on a gigantic scale.

By the 20th century, the limitations of that tradition were all too apparent. Its striving after sublimity was too often grandiose rather than grand. Today the Hudson River School attracts little interest outside the United States. Despite the wildness of its subjects, its adherence to earlier, European conventions makes it seem narrow and predictable.

Because Canada became a nation almost a hundred years after the United States, its great nationalist landscape tradition arose in the 20th century rather than the 19th. Like the painters of the Hudson River School, Tom Thomson and the Group of Seven sought a Canadian version of "that wilder image". They found it first in the Canadian Shield and later in the Canadian Rockies, the Arctic, and the Laurentians. The fact that they didn't discover it in the western prairies, or in the farmland and parkland which makes up most of inhabited, rural Canada, was in keeping with the practice of their American predecessors. Both movements sought the hand of God untainted by the hand of man.[4]

And, again like the Hudson River painters, they worked within European conventions. Only now the conventions were inherently modernist: Nabis-style, School of Paris Post-Impressionism, often gleaned, at second hand, from Scandinavian landscape painting and Art Nouveau design.

In the 1880s, advanced artists in Paris began to react against the seeming amorphousness of Impressionism. As they were unwilling to return to academic "finish", they introduced structure to their pictures by emphasizing linear, two-dimensional design. In the hands of Cézanne, this produced finished paintings which were something like grandly-organized sketches. But it led more commonly to a style which organized flattened, silhouetted shapes into bold designs. This style was developed in the 1880s by Van Gogh and Gauguin and in the 1890s by Toulouse-Lautrec, Edvard Munch, and the Nabis.

If Manet and the Impressionists were the first true modernists, the artists who simplified and rationalized modernism were these Post-Impressionists. Their boldly-organized paintings were deliberately and declaratively artificial, and seemed to break decisively with the representational basis of traditional, European painting. This quality of artifice gave figures in paintings by Van Gogh, Gauguin, and their followers a suggestive aura. It made them seem symbolic.

Symbolism was popular in the late 19th century, although it certainly wasn't confined to Post-Impressionism. But in more traditional, naturalistic painting, the environment provided confusing, cluttered settings for symbolic subjects. The symbol was at home on a flat surface. Post-Impressionism provided one.

By the early 20th century, Post-Impressionism's triumph was virtually complete. If its painting hadn't finally conquered (it still shocked England and America in 1912 and 1913), its design had. Modern printing and commercial illustration rapidly adopted the flat, page-oriented, Post-Impressionist design style, Art Nouveau. Most members of the Group of Seven were commercial artists. Where they weren't directly influenced by French Post-Impressionism (Arthur Lismer saw the Post-Impressionist exhibition Roger Fry organized for the Grafton Galleries in London in 1912; A. Y. Jackson studied in Paris), they learned it from Art Nouveau design.

This new, symbol-oriented style encouraged a new kind of literary painting which the Group of Seven adopted to portray a new image of Canada. The Group painted wild, natural scenery similar to that favoured by the Hudson River School, but painted it from a different historical vantage point. It couldn't render that scenery in the Hudson River School's terms.[5] The conventions which dominated its new art were drawn from the *fin de siècle*, art for art's sake, the "decadence" and — ultimately — from Post-Impressionism. The weathered pine tree in the wilderness and other flat, iconic symbols which dominated so many Group of Seven paintings suggested endurance and survival in a hostile, natural environment rather than awesomeness and sublimity.

And these images, like those of Lautrec, Bonnard and Munch in the 1890s, reproduced well. In fact, they often looked better in reproduction,[6] where their flatness looked less filled-in and their symbolism, reduced in scale, seemed more appropriate. The Group of Seven's long domination of Canadian art stems as much from this combination of reproducibility and nationalism as from its sheer, artistic achievement.

So the members of the Group of Seven were modernists as much as they were nationalists: modernist conventions dominated their painting; a modernist-inspired attitude governed their rejection of academic art. But modernism and nationalism weren't entirely compatible. Despite its French origins, modernist painting was an international phenomenon. Its insistence that works of art are self-contained, aesthetic objects which must be contemplated in a detached, disinterested manner made it difficult for nationalist aspirations to exist in relation to them. Certainly those aspirations could be embodied in works of art, but the fact that they would then be contemplated disinterestedly meant that the feelings they evoked couldn't be direct and gripping.[7] National images and aspirations had as much — and as little — place in paintings as rocks and trees or bottles and apples or, for that matter, paint and canvas.

Alternately, nations could point to artistic achievement itself as a source of national pride. France had done so with some justification. But achievement of that kind had to be established in an international and historical context — and international recognition isn't won easily.[8] In the late 19th and early 20th centuries, that recognition brought hundreds of foreign artists to France (A.Y. Jackson among them). By about 1920, "French" art was virtually dominated by the non-French.

Members of the Group of Seven faced the difficult task of reconciling a "pure" modernist art with an art designed to arouse nationalist sentiments. They reconciled it through various semi-mystical theories of nature and creativity, a practice which had been common in the arts since the Romantic era. But the conflict was never really resolved. The Group was never able to defend its beliefs convincingly in the face of criticism from succeeding generations of "purer" modernists. It ended up maintaining that its art owed nothing to "Europe" and disparaging the beliefs, if not always the art, of those whose work did. Its failure to resolve this conflict placed some of its artists in a position where they felt compelled to speak out against subsequent modernist developments in Canada.

But, ultimately, the estimation of its own art suffered as well. The Group of Seven's nationalism — not its modernism — created its public. And the very size and enthusiasm of that public weighed against the disinterested assessment of the art of its members. This isn't to say that this art was praised unduly — although it often was — but that it was praised for the wrong thing. As a result, the Group's achievements in painting have too often been overlooked.

Thomson and members of the Group of Seven all painted small oil sketches from nature, some of which they enlarged in their studios. In doing this, they encountered problems artists had struggled with for centuries. In the sketch, the hand relates comfortably and naturally to the medium, whether it's pencil, watercolour or oil paint. But when the sketch is enlarged, imagination must compensate for what the hand and the material can no longer supply easily and naturally. For artists like Poussin or Raphael, this meant constructing firm, monumental "space-compositions" which used architectural organization and theatrical situations to compensate for the loss of vitality brought about by increase in scale. In the 19th century — from about the time of Delacroix — imagination increasingly sought to enlarge the very "incompleteness" and spontaneity of the sketch. Artists literally sought ways to sketch large. This meant tackling easel paintings and studio paintings as though they were large sketches. For the most part, the Impressionists painted easel paintings from nature. Even when they didn't, when they worked-up studio paintings from sketches

and preliminary studies, they tended to keep the look of spontaneity in mind.

In enlarging smaller outdoor sketches in the studio, the Group didn't follow orthodox modernist practice. If anything, it did the reverse. Its practice wasn't derived from modernism, although its style was. Painters of the Group really worked in two modernist styles, a direct and colourful sketching style, and a rather cumbersome, Art Nouveau-influenced manner which almost invariably betrayed the inspiration of their sketches.

One of the most typical Group of Seven paintings depicted a lone, symbolic tree in the wilderness. Thomson's THE JACK PINE and THE WEST WIND are probably the most famous examples of this genre. They are both large, overdesigned, tapestry-like paintings, which have been reproduced extensively and have come, in the eyes of many Canadians, to stand for Canada as much as for Canadian art. Varley, Lismer, and Lawren Harris all produced their own versions. Of these, Varley's STORMY WEATHER, GEORGIAN BAY was the most successful.

Varley was probably the most gifted painter of the Group. He was a master draughtsman and paint handler, but this mastery was often undermined by his reliance on dark, iridescent colour. This kind of colour was rather fashionably decorative, as though Post-Impressionist simultaneous contrasts had been forced into the dark tonality of a Delacroix or Courbet. Nevertheless, Varley was one of the least doctrinaire members of the Group. He didn't just paint the landscape, but painted portraits as well, imbuing them with a kind of "transcendental" fervour, as though they were symbols of some higher, more sensuous reality.

Arthur Lismer's lone pine pictures, a series entitled SEPTEMBER GALE, GEORGIAN BAY, tended to be rather stiffly designed, as did most of his paintings of the 1920s and 1930s. The stiff, angular design which characterized his art during these decades was rather self-consciously modern. For all that this may have betrayed a leaning towards Cubism, it often appeared to be imposed upon his subjects. But in the 1940s and 1950s, his art was unexpectedly revitalized.

The paintings of these years were produced on Canada's seacoasts, and concentrated on subjects seen close-up: flotsam and jungle-like tangles of foliage from the Pacific Coast; dock litter from the Atlantic. These subjects enabled Lismer to draw freely, juxtaposing a variety of unlikely shapes and textures. Although these crowded, tangled paintings frequently failed — usually because they were too literal and too conventionally graphic, too drawn-and-then-coloured — when they did succeed, they demonstrated an inspired, personal vision.

Their kinship with Surrealism may have been influenced by Lismer's contact with contemporary American and European art during his sojourn as a professor of Art Education at Columbia University in New York during the winter of 1938-39. But whatever the influence, it seems to have been surprisingly beneficial, unlike the impulse, again an "international" one, which drove Lawren Harris to abstraction in his later years.

Surrealism was, in a sense, a last outburst of Art Nouveau symbolism. Not only did it stress the subconscious mind, the storehouse of symbols and archetypes, but it often rendered those symbols with a fluid, "organic" line, resurrected from the Art Nouveau arabesque. While its orientation toward the symbol was in keeping with the ideals of the Group, its tendency to draw those symbols from the subconscious mind made it too personal to awaken nationalist sentiments. But the national fought with the spiritual in the minds of some members of the Group. As a result, the later development of artists like Lismer, Harris, and Varley engaged international modernism in ways which compromised the nationalist tendencies of the Group.

Lawren Harris's paintings like NORTH SHORE, LAKE SUPERIOR and huge, iconic pictures of mountains made him seem the most abstract and "modern" painter of the Group of Seven, and he eventually turned to abstraction. But somehow, Harris's demonstratively "modern" art was undermined by his tendency to conceive broadly-painted, geometrical shapes which looked like grandiose stage sets when they were arranged in more or less naturalistic space. As a result, his paintings seemed to illustrate or dramatize the spiritual, without convincingly embodying it in paint. Nevertheless, Harris's spirituality, in combination with his self-conscious modernism, made his paintings enormously appealing. More than any other painter, he popularized the idea of modern art in Canada.

J. E. H. MacDonald was the elder statesman of the Group and, again, one of its better outdoor painters. While his sketches are some of the best produced by the Group, like the others he had difficulty translating them into a larger format. In paintings of the 1920s, like THE

SOLEMN LAND, tapestry-like patterning — possibly derived from Thomson — overwhelmed spatial recession. His large mountain paintings of the early 1930s are stifled by flat, hard-edged design and muddy colour. Despite this, his late sketches have a freshness and directness which are unique in the Group. Their freshness derives from an unusual reliance on light, clear colour. Unfortunately, however, he seems to have been unable to translate these qualities into large pictures. This was especially true of the paintings he produced in the mountains prior to his death in 1932. MacDonald seems to have been a uniquely-divided artist, even among members of the Group. His gift for translating natural subjects into clear, simplified, evocative designs was probably more prodigious than any of the others. If he learned this from Thomson, he applied it with even greater consistency and invention. But this gift seems to have abandoned him in the studio. More surprisingly still, it seems to have done so increasingly during his last years, at the very time his sketches were gaining in freshness and authority.

The Winnipeg painter, Lionel Lemoine FitzGerald, became a member of the Group of Seven in 1932, following J. E. H. MacDonald's death, and became a charter member of the Canadian Group of Painters in 1933, when the Group of Seven was dissolved. But FitzGerald, who had studied at the Art Students League in New York, was never a typical, Group of Seven-style nationalist. His mature works of the 1930s and 1940s are intimate and "pure", more in keeping with the concerns of the Contemporary Art Society in Montreal than of the Group. His art was deliberately modern and sometimes — although never very successfully — abstract. Like the art of his contemporary, David Milne, it succeeded most frequently on paper and on a modest scale.

A.Y. Jackson and Tom Thomson remain the most famous and representative members of the Group of Seven — despite the fact that Thomson died three years before the Group was officially formed. Thomson's big, iconic pictures and small, boldly painted sketches and Jackson's endless, undulating depictions of Canadian scenery set a standard — for better or for worse — against which Canadian art in this century has been judged. In addition to this, they influenced the attitude of

15

several generations of Canadians to their own countryside. Their land became our land.

They both became legendary Canadians. Thomson's reputation as a natural, untutored genius has made critical appraisal of his art difficult. While Jackson's painting is more commonly regarded as the work of a mere mortal, his artistic wanderings, in combination with his dedication to the Group of Seven's ideal, made him an enormously influential figure. With his vast circle of admirers and acquaintances scattered across the country, he did more to establish the influence and authority of the Group than any other person or institution. In this sense, he was unquestionably the most influential Canadian artist of the century.

In the long run, Jackson may be the better artist of the two. Certainly he had enormous advantages: he was the only French-trained painter of the Group; in addition to this, he was one of the few life-long, full-time painters of the Group — and he lived a longer life than the others. In terms of sheer productivity, he was something of a Canadian Monet. But, unlike Monet, he succeeded almost exclusively in small, on-the-spot sketches. It is in these sketches, supposedly Thomson's domain, that Jackson excelled.

Certainly his sketches weren't consistently good; certainly, too, his sketching style changed over the years. The crisp design and decorative colour accents of his sketches from the 1920s and 1930s gave way to a more fluid, painterly manner in his later years. These later sketches tended to be painted on slightly larger panels than the earlier ones. They were sometimes compromised by areas of dark, local colour which interrupted their surfaces and spatial continuity. But when Jackson's colour softened, when it greyed off and became more close-valued — when it became more "French" — his late sketches succeeded in a way that Thomson's most often did not.

Thomson wasn't quite the colourist he has been made out to be. His legendary boldness too often led him astray. His sketches were frequently torn apart by overstated contrasts, by hot tube colours interspersed with black or extremely dark colour, and by scumbled, *fin de siècle* iridescent effects. Exceptions existed — and magnificent ones, like his small sketch of FRASER'S LODGE — but usually these were assisted by some deterioration of, or exception to, the famous Thomson manner — when his stiff, angular brush-work gave way to more relaxed, fluid handling and, above all, when contrasts of value and hue gave way to softer, close-valued colour and relations of warm greys.

Thomson's art probably suffered as a result of his lack of exposure to European modernist painting. He seems to have learned too much from commercial design and too little from Jackson. And, in turn, his influence seems to have drawn Jackson away from his School of Paris manner into the undulating, linear approach which ruined so many of his studio paintings.

Jackson's sojourn in France made him a rather conservative modernist. He became a Post-Impressionist who venerated Impressionism and despised Cubism. But he must have imbibed something of the modernist sense of adventure — of making a new kind of art — and must have passed it on to Thomson.

Thomson wasn't the first Canadian Post-Impressionist. James Wilson Morrice preceded him by almost twenty years. But Morrice, despite his achievements, was an expatriate. He was a cosmopolitan, European painter, at home in the salons of Paris. Although he was Canadian-born, he saw Canada through European eyes. Thomson took the notion that modern art was new and bold, applied to it the Canadian North, and presented Canada with a bold, new image of itself. In doing so, he claimed Canada for modern art.

Terry Fenton

1. Donald Creighton, "Macdonald, Confederation and the West", *Historical Essays on the Prairie Provinces*, ed. Donald Swainson. (Toronto: McClelland and Stewart Ltd., 1970) pp. 69-70.

2. Joan Murray. *The Art of Tom Thomson* (Toronto: The Art Gallery of Ontario, 1971) pp. 27, 36.

3. It can be argued that history painting in France after the revolution was nationalist. But the revolutionary impulse of this painting led it to criticize the nation as much as glorify it. In England, some of Turner's naval pictures glorified the Empire — but his landscapes and "atmospheric" pictures didn't.

4. There were exceptions, notably A. Y. Jackson's paintings of rural Quebec. His depictions of old villages almost engulfed by snow-covered hills represent a culture which is so much a part of the environment it has become a kind of natural fact.

5. They were avid readers of Henry David Thoreau and Walt Whitman, writers whose sentiments paralleled those of the Hudson River School. But sentiment is one thing; style is another. Despite its literary leanings, the Group didn't take its style from literature.

6. Joan Murray, *The Art of Tom Thomson*, p. 7.

7. The presence of the *Tricolore* in many French, Post-Impressionist paintings suggests that, in their willingness to exploit the flag of France for sheerly aesthetic ends, French artists were insisting on this.

8. The international acclaim the Group of Seven received at Wembley didn't last. They used it to confirm their position as the Canadian establishment and to justify their modernism and nationalism within Canada.

Tom Thomson   *Fraser's Lodge (Mowat Lodge)*   oil on panel   8½"x10½"   1915   Edmonton Art Gallery

Tom Thomson   *The West Wind* (sketch)   oil on panel   8½″x10½″   1916   Ontario Heritage Foundation, Art Gallery of Ontario

A.Y. Jackson   *First Snow, Algoma*   oil on canvas   42″x50″   1919-20   McMichael Canadian Collection

J.E.H. MacDonald   *The Elements, Georgian Bay*   oil on board   28″x36⅛″   1916   Art Gallery of Ontario

Frank H. Johnston   *Fire-Swept, Algoma*   oil on canvas   50¼"x66"   1920   National Gallery of Canada

F.H. Varley   *Stormy Weather, Georgian Bay*   oil on panel   8½"x10½"   c.1920   McMichael Canadian Collection

J.E.H. MacDonald *Evening Light, Wheat Harvest* oil on board 8½"x10¼" 1931 Edmonton Art Gallery

Lawren Harris   *Athabasca Valley, Jasper Park*   oil on panel   10½″x13⅞″   1924   Edmonton Art Gallery

L.L. FitzGerald   *Apples, Still Life*   oil on masonite   12″x15″   1933   H.R. Milner Collection

Arthur Lismer   *Rock and Pine*   oil on canvas   32¼"x40½"   1935   Edmonton Art Gallery

L.L. FitzGerald *Prairie Landscape* watercolour 18"x24" 1941 Edmonton Art Gallery

Arthur Lismer   *Dock Litter*   oil on board   11½"x15½"   1952   H.R. Milner Collection

F.H. Varley   *The Cherry Tree*   oil on panel   12″x15″   undated   Edmonton Art Gallery

A.Y. Jackson   *View of South Pine Island, Go Home Bay*   oil on board   10½″x13½″   1966   The Downstairs Gallery

. . . That had made him think
about the noise in the city,
the noise that drove people
insane and filled the asylums,
and yet he had admitted to
himself the futility of trying to
escape into the woods.
"Whatever is to be done
culturally, creatively,
economically will be done
in the city. Whatever is to rise
up from the ashes of the old
American world will have its
growth in the city . . . Maybe
I can't appreciate from here
how grand this country is
with the rocks and the lake
and the hills . . . You know
what I'd like? I'd love to see
a newspaper every
morning . . ." [1]
Peter Gould in
A Broken Journey
by Morley Callaghan, 1932.

Montreal in the 1930s and the Contemporary Art Society

The conflict between modernist painters in Montreal and the Group of Seven dominated Canadian art during the 1930s. In theory, it was similar to the earlier struggle between the Group of Seven and the Canadian establishment; but, in fact, it was not. The Group of Seven met with only token opposition. If the 19th century Dutch painting which Jackson deplored was the art some wealthy Canadians preferred to collect, it was hardly the art Canadian artists and intellectuals admired. It wasn't very original — and it was foreign.

In the 1920s and 1930s, many of the best Canadian artists were expatriates. James Wilson Morrice, the Canadian Post-Impressionist who introduced French modernism to Montreal, died in Tunis in 1924. David Milne returned from the U.S. in 1929, settling in Ontario. John Lyman returned to Montreal from France in 1931. Alfred Pellan returned from France in 1940.

Lyman's return was particularly important: he brought his experience of French modernism to Montreal. At that time, French modernism, in all its manifestations, was dominated by the non-French — Picasso, Gris, Soutine, Chagall, and Lipchitz — and could hardly claim to be narrowly nationalistic. Even in its most "French" manifestation, in the art of Matisse and his circle which Lyman introduced to Montreal, it was inherently and unredeemably international.

The 1930s was a critical decade for the nation state and nationalism. National economies foundered in a prolonged depression; aggressively nationalistic fascist dictorships arose in Italy, Spain, and Germany; massive unemployment and starvation wages shook the foundations of North American society. During that decade, the nationalist aspirations of the Group of Seven began to seem increasingly irrelevant to ambitious painters in Montreal. In promoting national identity, Group of Seven painting had been a means to an end. Painters in Montreal thought painting should be an end in itself and openly aligned their art with the School of Paris. In doing so, they questioned the authority and relevance of the Group. In the face of this growing dissatisfaction, the Group of Seven disbanded in 1933 and reformed as the much larger Canadian Group of Painters. This new organization proposed to consolidate Canadian painting in the face of the recent inroads made by the School of Paris. "Modernism in Canada," it maintained in the catalogue of its first exhibition, "has almost no relation to the modernism of Europe." [2]

Canadian painters weren't alone in this reaction to Europe. In the United States, the American Scene painters fought a similar fight at the same time with similar rhetoric. But it was similar only to a point. The American Scene movement wasn't the first nationalist painting movement in America. Its painters weren't interested in wilderness landscape like their 19th century predecessors in the Hudson River School. They preferred to paint the American people. But while their populist beliefs led to (or were provoked by) their rejection of Parisian modernism, theirs remained a modernist-influenced art if only because of their place in history. Like the Group of Seven, they adopted the simplified design and generalized forms of late 19th century modernism virtually without question. And, again like the Group, they deplored the inherent internationalism and supposed abandonment of "content" of more recent modernist painting. They appropriated some modernist, formal conventions and applied them to unrelated, literary themes and situations.

So, while the Group of Seven wasn't a populist movement, its reaction to French modernism was coloured by the same prejudices which consumed the American Scene. Its reaction was a form of isolationism in the face of the political turmoil in Europe. European civilization itself seemed bankrupt. French modernism, as a product of that civilization, seemed to threaten the moral authority of the New World.

The internationalist position was expounded primarily by John Lyman. Although he established the Contemporary Art Society to consolidate it, he spoke for an attitude toward art rather than for a specific group of painters. This entailed criticizing some of the fundamental beliefs of the Group of Seven. The controversy which resulted polarized the Canadian art world. If Lyman spoke through Montreal newspapers, the Group responded by entrenching their control of public and private patronage. This was made possible, in large part, by the enormous influence of A. Y. Jackson. The National Gallery of Canada continued to support the Group until the 1940s, and most public galleries in Canada followed suit. So Lyman's cause was defeated.

As a result, time has not adequately salvaged the achievement of Lyman and other members of the Contemporary Art Society. His failure to establish the credibility of his position and his art in Canada has echoed down to the present. Perhaps he was unwise to insist upon it. In making an aesthetic quarrel public, he may have polarized an art scene which was too frail to bear it. The Group and their supporters might otherwise have accommodated Parisian internationalism of the 1930s. Certainly they had embraced French modernism for the sake of their own art two decades earlier.

In any event, internationally-oriented modernism was dealt a blow from which it didn't recover until after the Second World War. Although the Contemporary Art Society was formed to provide a kind of organized opposition to the Group of Seven-sponsored Canadian Group of Painters, it never achieved wide recognition. Artists like Lyman himself, Goodridge Roberts, Philip Surrey, and Louis Muhlstock languished in comparative obscurity. But their contribution to Canadian art is undeniable. They established a modernist art in Canada which sought recognition on the basis of its own, intrinsic quality.

The Frenchness of the Contemporary Art Society didn't stem from Cubism; nor was it entirely Fauvist. Although it stemmed from Matisse rather than Picasso, it was more purely post-Impressionist than post-Fauve, despite the fact that it drew upon Fauvism's clear, heightened colour. Above all, it stemmed from theory — in the relative absence of experience.

The theory came primarily from the writings of the French-oriented English critics, Roger Fry and Clive Bell. It maintained that paintings are self-contained, aesthetic objects, the experience of which is supra-national. National boundaries, it maintained, have no influence on taste. [3]

To Fry and Bell, Post-Impressionism was modernist art *per se.* In their view, it was an art — produced since Impressionism — which emphasized design over and above naturalistic representation. But this design was still conceived to be a force which organized, and grew out of, the visible world. Fry, in particular, believed that representation was necessary, that it provided "forms" which could be organized into complex designs to make pictures. He didn't believe that imagination, of itself, could conceive the kind of vital and appropriate forms demanded by pictorial art. In his opinion, it was presumptuous and, above all, unfruitful to reject, or "improve on", nature.

Fry wasn't alone — or even narrowly English — in this. Renoir believed it (if we are to believe his son, Jean), as had, presumably, most of the great French painters of the late 19th century. Even Picasso believed it. But Miro — at least in Fry's opinion — departed from it. Surrealism, perhaps especially as exemplified by Miro, was anathema to Fry. The idea that good painting could be generated by "ideography, symbolism, expressionism"[4] seemed impossible.

For all his belief in design — in the formal, non-representational aspect of art — Fry didn't think it could produce high art in and of itself. Certainly he had some reason to feel this way. At the time, non-objective art had achieved little. Even Cubism synthesized forms from nature. Fry observed once that the purest kind of painting was still-life painting. To him, it existed most exclusively for the sake of formal relations — for art's sake. French painting seemed to approach all subjects in that spirit. And Post-Impressionist painters in Montreal followed suit.

Their Frenchness, then, wasn't the adoption of an alien, nationalist manner; on the contrary, it represented an alignment with the most declaratively international art of the day. It was French the way painting in Bloomsbury was French. It drew particularly on Cézanne and Matisse. In some respects, it was an enlargement and distillation of the Group of Seven's sketching style. Forms were simplified and generalized and, occasionally, heightened in colour. Value contrasts — in opposition to Group of Seven practice — tended to be suppressed.

The most significant English-Canadian painters in Montreal during the 1930s and 1940s were John Lyman and Goodridge Roberts. Lyman, the senior member of the Contemporary Art Society, worked in simplified, bulging contours which suggested simple volumes. But these volumes, with their complex references to depth, provided an awkward framework for colour. Lyman's colour was light, saturated, and clear. Its very clarity — clearer and more brilliant, it seemed, than nature — called for more radically-flattened drawing and layout than Lyman was willing to provide. As a result, his paintings are often upset or overwhelmed by a high-pitched, strident intensity which seems at odds with the rather classical balance of their compositions. Ironically, A. Y. Jackson — Lyman's great nationalist opponent — is generally a superior painter, if only because his muddied, atmospheric colour is more thoroughly French.

The younger Montreal painters (apart from Stanley Cosgrove, whose landscapes and still lifes of the 1940s gravitated to Cubist-derived earth colours and a kind of flat, schematic drawing reminiscent of Braque) worked in manners which ranged from Lyman's modelled rendering to a flatter, more painterly manner perfected by Goodridge Roberts. Roberts was the supreme painter of the group, and many of the others — Jori Smith, Louis Muhlstock, and Philip Surrey among them — are at their best when they approach his painterly directness.

Like David Milne, Roberts studied in New York at the Art Students League. But he was influenced primarily by French painting, particularly by the immediately pre-Fauve Matisse. The subject, handling, and colour of Matisse's CARMELINA (presently in the Museum of Fine Arts in Boston) looks like a model for Roberts' many interiors with female nudes. That painting reduces modelling to loosely-brushed passages which have the autonomy of local colour and, because of their flatness and directness, declare the picture surface with a new (for 1903) immediacy. Roberts, like many English painters of the

1920s (Duncan Grant, Vanessa Bell, and even Roger Fry) and like the French "gentle Fauve", Albert Marquet, made a career of painting in this manner. His was an art devoted to sheer aesthetic experience. It ignored the Canadian North. Its subjects were frequently drawn from cultivated, middle-class, urban life. It was neither elitist nor effete. It revelled in and exalted the familiar in interiors, still lifes and landscapes.

This kind of painting was Roger Fry's Post-Impressionism *par excellence*. In reaction, perhaps, to the Group of Seven, Roberts adapted it to the Canadian landscape — particularly to marginally agricultural land and rolling parkland, to summer vacation country rather than untamed, northern wilderness. Even his Georgian Bay paintings of the 1950s reveal a Georgian Bay which has become accessible to the summer vacationer. But, whatever their orientation, his remain some of the most eloquent Canadian paintings of this century.

To Jackson and the Group of Seven (and the Canadian Group of Painters), this French, "aesthetic" approach to Canadian painting represented a willingness to settle for less, to be provincial followers rather than innovators. And there was some reason for this objection. Despite the Montreal painters' insistence that aesthetic experience couldn't be limited by accidents of geography, their art was. They produced a Canadian-flavoured version of an international style. They weren't great painters. Most likely, they didn't presume to be. Certainly their art didn't break new ground internationally. It broke ground in Canada that had been broken earlier in Paris.

But that was true, equally, of the art of the Group of Seven. They too were modernists. They too broke ground only in Canada. But they tried to claim a special status for their achievement, maintaining that a "rugged", "uncultivated" art was, necessarily, more Canadian — and therefore superior — to one which succumbed to "European" cultivation.

The woodsman, the rugged individualist, the refugee from "civilization", has often been lionized in North America — sometimes justifiably. But escape from civilization doesn't necessarily produce aesthetic, intellectual, or moral integrity. All too often it has produced the opposite. And when its effect has been beneficial, that benefit has stemmed largely from the survival and growth of "civilized" values of one kind or another.

In choosing Europe during the 1930s and 1940s, modernist painters in Montreal demonstrated that European, urban life had something of value to offer Canadians, perhaps something more "useful" than what had been provided by images of a forbidding, northern wilderness. So, if their art didn't triumph, their philosophy — in a quiet way — did. For all their attachment to nature, Canadians have become — of necessity — a cultivated, urban people. In the long run, despite their involvement with the North, they have become more and more fundamentally attached to the values proclaimed by the Contemporary Art Society. Granted, the image of cultivation is less appealing than the image of solitude, independence, and survival in the face of a hostile environment. But cultivation calls for real independence, entails real solitude, and survives always against great adversity — as the acceptance of the Contemporary Art Society has demonstrated. Canadians still cling to old myths.

Terry Fenton

1. Morley Callaghan, *A Broken Journey* (Toronto: Macmillan of Canada, 1932), pp. 195-196.

2. See Dennis Reid, *A Concise History of Canadian Painting*, Oxford University Press (Canadian branch), 1973, p. 174. Significantly, this first exhibition was held in Atlantic City, New Jersey. The American art scene, at that time, didn't pose a threat to Canadian art. The CGP identified formalism (or its 1930s equivalent) with Europe, not America.

3. The remarkable similarity between paintings by members of the Contemporary Art Society and English painters of the 1920s and 1930s (particularly the Bloomsbury group) suggests the influence of the ideas and attitudes of Fry and Bell. John Lyman's and Goodridge Roberts' paintings are remarkably similar to those of Duncan Grant, Vanessa Bell and Roger Fry, himself. Roberts' paintings, in particular, recall those of the English modernist, Matthew Smith, who, like John Lyman, studied briefly with Matisse.

4. See *The Letters of Roger Fry*, ed. Denys Sutton, (London: Chatto and Windus, 1972) pp. 567-568. In contradiction to this opinion, Fry was equally offended by the blatantly sexual imagery he found in Klee and Miro.

John Lyman   *La Plage à St. Jean de Luz*   oil on canvas   17¾″x21½″   1926   Dominion Gallery

Adrien Hébert   *Place St. Henri*   oil on canvas   26″x30″   1929   Art Gallery of Hamilton

Alfred Pellan   *Le Panier Bouclé*
oil on canvas   45½"x35"   1933
National Gallery of Canada

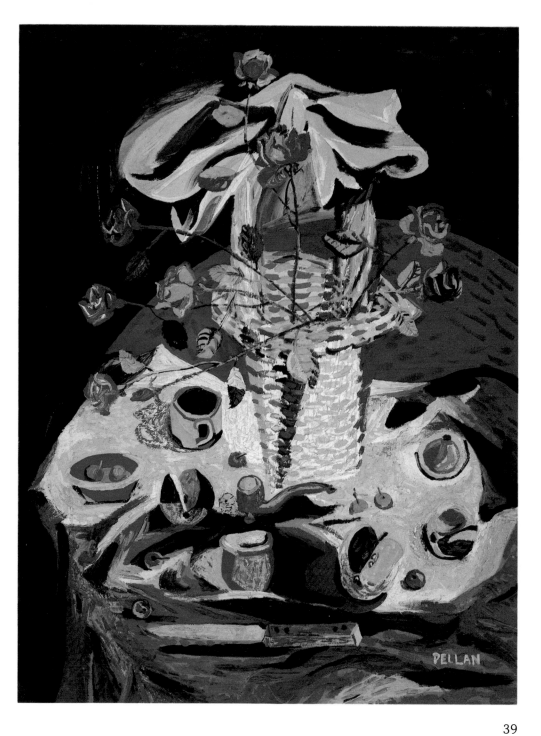

Goodridge Roberts
The Lady in the Green Hat   oil on canvas
21″x15¾″   1936   Edmonton Art Gallery

Louis Muhlstock
Empty Rooms   oil on canvas
30-1/16"x25-1/16"   1938
Edmonton Art Gallery

Goodridge Roberts *Late Afternoon St. Alphonse* oil on canvas 22"x26" 1942 Dr & Mrs William H. Lakey

Philip Surrey   *The French Novel*   oil on panel   12″x16″   1944   Edmonton Art Gallery

Stanley Cosgrove   *Green Forest, Large Landscape*   oil on masonite   38″x46″   1950   Dominion Gallery

Jori Smith   *Vitaline*   oil on board
23¾"x18⅞"   1952
Dominion Gallery

Two Isolated Modernists

David Milne *The Ski Jump* oil on canvas 16x22⅛" 1927 Edmonton Art Gallery

David Milne   *Studio Interior*   watercolour   14½"x20½"   c.1940   H.R. Milner Collection

Emily Carr *Forest Interior*
oil on paper   22″x16″   undated
J.A. MacAulay

Emily Carr   *Strait of Juan de Fuca*   oil on paper   22⅛″x34¼″   undated   Edmonton Art Gallery

Milne's modernist principles, perhaps in combination with his lack of hostility toward the Group of Seven, established his reputation in Canada as a kind of artist's artist. Whether that reputation was justified is debatable. He was an original artist and, at best, a very good one. But his art was compromised by its very intimacy, by its mannered drawing, simplified, preconceived colour, and relative confinement to watercolour. His very purity and "compression" may, in the long run, have restricted his vision.

David Milne returned to Canada in 1929, having spent the first twenty-five years of his career in the United States. He had studied under Maurice Prendergast at the Art Students League in New York in the early 20th century, was a young modernist in New York before World War I, and was the only Canadian painter to be represented in the famous New York Armory Show in 1913. A Prendergast-influenced Post-Impressionist, he excelled in rather modest works, mostly watercolours and small oils.

He developed his own version of the silhouette style of the 1890s. His paintings are a kind of adorned drawing — flat and schematic and almost affectedly childlike. His hand was governed by a highly-sophisticated wrist. His drawing was highly stylized, as was his colour, which was chosen primarily for its sheer decorative effect. Milne tended to preconceive colour, often producing three- and four-colour pictures, to increase the impact of his simplified design.

Although Milne admired the paintings of some members of the Group of Seven, he was not interested in their nationalist aspirations. Apart from the fact that he had lived outside Canada for so long, he was, first and foremost, an artist for art's sake. He used motifs for the sake of their forms rather than for the ideas and attitudes symbolized by them. Although he lived during the 1930s in the wilderness at Six Mile Lake on the Severn River in Northern Ontario — and was more of an outdoorsman than some members of the Group — his work never strived after grandeur or symbolic statement. He seems to have looked upon nature as a haven from civilization and, most of all, as an inexhaustible source of picture motifs.

Emily Carr has usually been represented as a west coast and women's representative of the Group of Seven sensibility. In a way, she was. She became a great admirer of their work — especially of Lawren Harris's, which she admired for its "spirituality". But her mature art wasn't at all like theirs. It was more resolutely modern — and more emphatically original.

During her studies in England and France, she worked in a modified Impressionist manner, employing somewhat heightened colour. Later, in Brittany, she painted darker, more linear pictures, drawn from village life, which anticipated her concerns in Canada. Upon her return in 1912, she began to document west coast Indian villages in oil paintings and watercolours. She felt a strong kinship with the native people and their art, and attempted to capture something of the primitive, iconic quality of their totems in relation to their natural settings. While some of these pictures — especially the watercolours — are superb, frequently the effect she intended was simply described, rather than embodied.

In the 1920s, she met some members of the Group of Seven, as well as the Seattle-based American modernist, Mark Tobey. Tobey seems to have had an extraordinary influence on her work. He had been to France, was familiar with Cubism, and had a rare ability to analyze and reconceive formal qualities of art. He visited Carr several times during the late 1920s and came to Victoria in 1928 to conduct a three-week study session for her and three other painters. This session prefigured the Emma Lake Artists' Workshops which took place in Saskatchewan three decades later. Presumably as a result of Tobey's influence, Carr's village pictures of 1928-31 displayed a new

Cubist-derived geometrical patterning. This evolved into her mature style, which began in 1932 when she began to paint studies of the B.C. rain forest in oil paint, diluted with gasoline, on large sheets of paper. She had always drawn more directly and naturally than she had coloured. The contrived, self-consciously "modern" look of her earlier pictures was replaced by a compelling, more radical manner which combined calligraphy and depiction. Now painting itself became drawing. These late works are composed entirely of writhing, undulating, curling, and zigzagging lines. Accumulations of this continuous drawing carried colour and nervous "spiritual" energy throughout the pictures. Although they were produced when she was in her sixties and seventies, they remain some of the most direct and expressive — and absolutely original — Canadian paintings of this century.

Although they have both come to be regarded as important national artists, David Milne and Emily Carr benefitted substantially from contact with an American art world which was becoming more and more deeply involved with French modernism. Milne's writings about art reveal a sophisticated and dedicated modernist sensibility. He was a "formal" artist in the best and worst senses. While he did not let irrelevant notions about the purpose of art interfere with his own practice, too often his vision seems constrained, rather than released, by formal conventions.

Convention stifled Emily Carr's early work to an even greater extent. But she was able, in her last years, to turn her isolation and spiritual yearnings into powerful, affecting art. This was a prodigious accomplishment. Spiritual yearnings have been part and parcel of some of the worst, most pretentious art of the past century and a half. And they have been particularly prevalent in provincial situations. Paris and New York have not tended to be centres of speculation about the spiritual in art. The main spiritually-oriented art theories came from Mondrian and Kandinsky rather than from Picasso and Matisse. In the provinces, artists are more isolated and, literally, more lonely. In that situation, spiritual and literary art theories may help justify an activity which, in a hostile or apathetic community, might otherwise seem virtually pointless.

Emily Carr's isolation was extreme. That she was able to turn it to advantage, albeit with the help of Mark Tobey and some members of the Group of Seven, was something of a miracle.

Terry Fenton

53

"Surrealism aims at the creation of a poetic world without limits, a world never seen before. It is necessary to invent something, a different world."[1]

Alfred Pellan

Montreal and the Collective Unconscious

Compared to the great adventures of the past, the discoveries of the 20th century seem intensely practical and prosaic. Despite Jacques Cousteau's forays into undersea depths, the romantic 19th century notion of penetrating unexplored continents no longer exists in its traditional sense. Our own century has substituted technological and scientific frontiers, but extraordinary as modern ventures into the unknown may be, a NASA countdown lacks the exoticism of Livingstone in the African jungle. Nevertheless, there is one 20th century expedition into *terra incognita* which enters a jungle as impenetrable as anything Livingstone encountered: the unmapped landscape of the human mind. Freud's theories are perhaps less dramatic than a live televised moon walk, but the ideas of the explorers of the psyche have had a profound and far-reaching effect on most aspects of 20th century life. This influence has extended to the arts, and has been reflected with particular clarity in painting and sculpture from the 1920s to the present.

The world of the 1920s was very different from that of the period before World War I. The cataclysm of the war destroyed a long-established social order. Life was irrevocably changed; previous assumptions were questioned, in the arts no less than anywhere else.

In Europe, the period immediately preceding World War I had seen remarkably vigorous activity in painting, especially in the work of Matisse and the Fauves, and Picasso and the Cubists. Around and immediately after World War I, the steady push towards abstraction which had characterized art from about 1875 seemed to falter, to be replaced by a more literary approach. Although the pioneers, Picasso and Matisse and their colleagues,

continued their formal investigations, many younger artists seemed dissatisfied by their kind of cerebral detachment. The Expressionists appropriated Fauve color and Cubist structure, but used them to suggest violence done to their subject matter, not as ends in themselves; the Dadaists were frankly hostile to traditional art of any sort, and delighted in shocking anti-aesthetic gestures. Rational ordering and structuring, so important to the artists of the pre-World War I period, seemed particularly antithetical to a group centered around André Breton which became known as the Surrealists. Surrealism seized upon Freudian theories of the mind's workings and made them central to a new aesthetic, described by Breton in the Surrealist Manifesto of 1924 as "pure psychic automatism, by which one intends to express verbally, in writing or by any other method, the real functioning of the mind".[2] Earlier, Breton had explained psychic automatism as a state "which corresponds rather closely to the state of dreaming".[3]

It was a cult of personal emotions, based on the belief that an individual's interior images and interior dialogue could be subject matter for works of art, since the dictates of the subconscious were as important and interesting as those of consciousness. Surrealism wasn't originally a movement of the visual arts, but of literature and philosophy. At the time of the 1924 Manifesto, there was no such thing as Surrealist painting. Painting seemed a contradiction of the movement's principles, since it involved actual forms and pre-supposed arrangement, formal detachment, manipulation and decision-making. "Pure psychic automatism" seemed to preclude this kind of conscious structuring, but eventually even the orthodox conceded that Surrealist pictures could exist. Automatism came to be seen as a way of releasing creativity, a kind of free association of ideas, sounds, images, or symbols. Applied to literature, it was "stream of consciousness" writing; in the visual arts, it became sophisticated doodling supposedly done without the dictates of conscious mind. Intended to free the artist from established habits of composing and image making, automatic drawing was presumed to release images and forms peculiar to the maker of the drawing. The principle of "poetic dislocation" or "metaphoric displacement" was closely related to automatism, substituting chance relationships for logical ones; things seen in surprising and illogical contexts, like dream images, were thought to gain in meaning.

No matter what his method, the Surrealist artist began not with a perception of visible reality, but with a conception of interior reality. Unlike the Fauves and the Cubists, who used perceptions of the real world as a basis for formal invention, the Surrealists used formal means — like automatic drawing — as a method of self-discovery. The mind's eye replaced the painter's eye, but the Surrealist painter was a figurative artist, presenting naturalistic representations of unnatural things. What we commonly think of as Surrealist art — Dali's "hand-painted dream photographs", for example — could be described as the "realist" side of the movement. In spite of the hallucinatory nature of the images, they are traditional in modelling and space, and in emphasis on subject matter. The "abstract" side of Surrealism — exemplified by Matta and Masson — presents ambiguous delirium images, yet even though what is represented cannot be verified in terms of actuality, we are still in the realm of art chiefly as representation.

From our present point of view, post-World War II art in the United States seems to revive the concerns of pre-World War I French art; Surrealism seems merely a brief aberration, irrelevant to earlier, more radical movements. Certainly it seems irrelevant to what came after, the abstract art of the period from the 1940s to the present. Paradoxically, while the *look* of "traditional" Surrealist art had little influence on subsequent movements, Surrealist ideas and attitudes have had a profound effect upon the art of the past thirty years. In Canada, they are central to the short-lived but vital movement, "Les Automatistes".

The Paris-based Surrealist movement flourished during the 1920s and continued through the difficult 1930s, publishing manifesti, exhibiting, and soliciting new converts to the faith. Paris was still the center of the art world, to which

artists from everywhere else looked for direction. Information about Paris came from magazines such as the influential *Cahiers d'art*, or more directly in New York through the newly founded Museum of Modern Art, or teachers such as Hans Hofmann. But for North Americans, French art belonged to a world which was distant, albeit infinitely desirable. In a very short time, however, this changed. The outbreak of World War II and the invasion of France by Germany caused many French artists (mostly Surrealists) to flee to the United States. What had seemed remote suddenly became part of daily experience.

The proximity of good European moderns had a catalytic effect on the younger New York artists of the 1940s and undoubtedly accelerated the development of American art. Conversely, the relative isolation of young Canadian artists made their development more difficult.

The 1930s in Canada saw a polarization of isolationist, regionally-oriented artists, centred around the Toronto based Group of Seven, and internationally-oriented artists instrumental in transmitting information about European art when he returned to Canada in 1931 after an absence of almost 24 years. An associate of Matisse, Lyman introduced a generation of Montreal artists to new ideas about what a work of art could be. In 1939, he helped found the Contemporary Art Society, which organized group exhibitions and functioned as an information centre. But despite the Society's efforts, Montreal's exposure to challenging European art remained limited. The Contemporary Art Society's "Art In Our Day" exhibition, held in 1939, included works by Derain, Dufy, Kandinsky, Marc, Modigliani, Utrillo, and Vlaminck. Since this was the Canadian equivalent of the Armory Show which introduced the European avant-garde to New York in 1913, it offers some indication of why Canadian art remained conservative. Nevertheless, the annual exhibitions of the C.A.S. showed work by some of the most adventurous artists in Canada.

These were a group of extremely young French-speaking painters, the students and associates of Paul-Emile Borduas, a Lyman protégé who helped run the Contemporary Art Society. (He became its director in 1948.) Because they were French-speaking, they had direct access to French Surrealist writings (they corresponded with Breton) and seized upon automatism as the central idea of their aesthetic.

For some, automatism seems to have been an end in

itself, often resulting in tempestuous, densely painted canvases which suggest that the painting is simply a visible record of a series of gestures. Others arrive at a more traditional Surrealist imagery of biomorphic forms in indeterminate space. The young Montrealers were, in either case, firmly committed to abstraction.

Unlike New York in the 1940s. Montreal was not encouraging to new art, and the group, which included Pierre Gauvreau, Marcel Barbeau, Jean-Paul Mousseau, Jean-Paul Riopelle, Fernand Leduc, Marcelle Ferron, and Borduas, held their exhibitions in borrowed apartments. Rare exceptions were the Borduas exhibitions at the Dominion Gallery, which also housed the annual C.A.S. show and the short-lived "Saggitaires" exhibition which included Borduas and his circle.

Equally rare were occasions to see important contemporary art or contacts with good European modern artists. Breton visited Canada, but made no effort to meet the young artists with whom he had corresponded, although after an initial meeting with Leduc in New York in 1945, Breton became a supporter of the Montreal group and an admirer of Borduas. In 1943, Léger was in Montreal, lecturing and showing the film "Le Ballet Mécanique"; a year later, an exhibition at the Montreal Museum of Fine Arts included paintings by Van Gogh and Mondrian. Some of the young Montrealers travelled to New York, for direct experience of contemporary works, while information at one remove was supplied by Louise Renaud, a member of the Borduas circle, employed by the Pierre Matisse family in 1944. The Pierre Matisse Gallery was by then the centre of Surrealist activity in New York, so that Mlle. Renaud's supply of news and critical reviews would have been of special interest.

(One can only speculate how much influence this connection had. Certainly curious relationships exist. The 1942 Surrealist exhibition in New York installed paintings in an elaborate web of ropes designed by Marcel Duchamp. Photographs show a seemingly random, complex arrangement, creating a transparent labyrinth through which the viewer had to move to examine the paintings. In 1947, Riopelle and Mousseau showed their recent work in a borrowed Montreal apartment. The walls were covered with dark material and the paintings hung on an arrangement of cords, rather like a volleyball net. It is tempting to see the Montreal exhibition as an attempt to echo the New York installation.)

"The Surrealists have revealed to us the moral importance of the unpremeditated act".[4]
Paul-Emile Borduas.

Recognition was slow in coming, in spite of some critical enthusiasm and small victories against the rigid, academic Ecole des Beaux Arts. Perhaps in an effort to reach a more sympathetic audience, in 1946 members of the Borduas circle showed a group of works in a dance studio in New York. By 1947, the group had shown frequently in a variety of improvised galleries (and some legitimate ones) and had been christened the *Automatistes*, after the title of a Borduas painting. In 1948, the Automatistes published their most controversial and influential manifesto, *Refus global*. The title essay was by Borduas, a passionate cry for individual freedom and independence of expression. An Existential declaration of personal responsibility for one's actions, *Refus global* was militantly anti-clerical, accusing the Church of perpetuating ignorance and repression in French Canada. Response to the manifesto was predictably violent. Borduas was immediately dismissed as a teacher at the Ecole du Meuble, while efforts of members of the intellectual community to rally support were completely unsuccessful.

Opposition to the Automatistes came chiefly from the clergy and from politicians, not from the artistic community, but shortly before the publication of *Refus global*, an anti-Automatiste faction united, published its own manifesto, *Prisme d'yeux*, and held an exhibition later that year. The *Prisme d'yeux* group declared itself for pure painting, free of ideological restrictions or literary, political, or philosophical overtones, yet the paintings of Alfred Pellan and Léon Bellefleur, central figures of the group, seem closely related to the Surrealist-inspired paintings of the Automatistes. Pellan had worked in France for a long time, returning to Montreal in 1940 to escape World War II. Although strongly influenced by the Synthetic Cubist paintings of Picasso, he knew the Surrealists, admired Breton, and had adopted automatist methods. His opposition to the Montreal Automatistes stemmed from a belief that automatism as an end in itself was too easy; for him automatic drawing was a means only of starting a picture. The artist's role, according to Pellan, was then to define and "humanize" the resulting images, to rescue them from the anonymity of abstraction and make them look like art. Pellan's associate, Bellefleur (who later switched to the Borduas camp), was so committed to Surrealist ideas that he participated in several "exquisite corpse" sessions, joint projects originally invented by the French Surrealists, which resulted in collective Surrealist drawings-cum-poems.

It is easy to understand how Montreal's French-speaking artists assimilated the ideology of the European Surrealists, and to see how the application of these theories, whether as an end in themselves or as a means of generating images, would result in paintings with similar characteristics. In addition to this literary or ideological influence, the look of abstract Surrealist painting, along with Picasso's paintings of the 1930s, seems to have been influential among many Canadian artists in the 1940s, who combined spiky images, derived from Synthetic Cubism, with biomorphic forms and illusionistic space derived from the Surrealists.

For other Canadians, the influences seem to have been visual rather than ideological, so that the persistence of Picasso-inspired forms probably result from the limited access Canadian artists had at the time to works offering alternative solutions. Some of the Montreal Automatistes arrived at an all-over format, markedly different from the closed Cubist space of many of their contemporaries. It seems to result logically from the Surrealist-derived conviction that the individual's way of making marks is the most significant aspect of the picture. Since each stroke was dictated by inner urgings, each stroke is a valid record of the promptings of the unconscious and therefore is no more important than any other. The resulting equalization of emphasis over the entire surface of the picture creates the Automatistes' densely textured all-over painting.

As in the United States, the Surrealists' legacy irrevocably changed the course of Canadian painting. The Automatistes have been called the first *modern* Canadian painters, a claim which can be supported both by their commitment to abstraction and their international aspirations. The movement was regrettably short-lived; Riopelle and Leduc left for France before the publication of *Refus global*, and Borduas, after a brief stay in New York, followed them to Paris. Nevertheless, the movement had proved the possibility of Canadian art which derived its Canadianness from the character of the people who made it, not from the characteristics of the Canadian landscape. After the long domination of the Group of Seven, this was no mean achievement.

"If I am certain that I am in front of a Mousseau, it is because of an unintentional plastic relationship, fatal and constant to Mousseau, which my memory recalls to me as something unique and particular to everything which he makes."[5]

Paul-Emile Borduas

With the emergence of Abstract Surrealism, and the development of Abstract Expressionism, which followed, it became clear that for the first time in history the centre of energy and innovation in the art world had shifted from the Old World to the New. Robert Motherwell has suggested that what is particularly North American about the art produced in this period is its violence,[6] but at the same time, it is apparent that post-World War II art in North America continues many of the concerns of pre-World War I French art. The literary content of Surrealism has been made subservient to non-associative, formal concerns. Nevertheless, many attitudes central to contemporary art derive from Surrealist theories.

In spite of Surrealism's apparent formal conservatism, the movement was deeply committed to the idea of originality, of setting about making something new. Earlier artists do not seem to have shared this obsession: Manet's famous statement that he wished "neither to overthrow earlier painting nor to make it new", but wished simply to be himself, seems typical. Dada's scorn for art in general and its genial nose-thumbing at tradition must have helped pave the way for the Surrealists' rejection of the known and deliberate pursuit of the unpredictable. The danger, of course, lies in newness being valued for its own sake and in originality being confused with novelty, but the concept of the artist striving to surprise both himself and his public is very much with us today.

Equally relevant to today's art is the Surrealist belief that the work of art is an extension of a particular (gifted) person. It is part of Surrealist doctrine that an individual's way of putting paint on canvas and his personal will to form are significant, simply because they are expressions of that individual. It is an essentially anti-academic belief, since academic art aspires to pre-established standards of excellence, not to revelations of previously unthought-of possibilities. Most present-day art is about art, not about the unconscious, but the fact that a Jack Bush looks different from a Charles Gagnon and that both are recognized as valid images, is related to Surrealist faith.

The idea of allowing the image to develop as it is painted, rather than beginning with a preconceived notion, is current among many artists today. This practice can be seen as a legacy of automatism. Similarly, the conceptual movement, in which the idea of the work of art is deemed sufficient as a statement, would have pleased André Breton mightily. His original conception of automatism was as a means of self-discovery. A work of art which had no other existence than the mind of its creator, or a description, is a logical result of Surrealist practice, the ultimate translation of self-expression into art.

Whatever the present state of Surrealist and surrealizing art, the movement's North American legacy is considerable. The presence of the Surrealists helped North American artists value themselves as the equals of the much admired Europeans. The ideas of the Surrealists reinforced this new sense of worth by stressing the importance of art as individual self-expression. These ideas, it appears, have not yet been exhausted.

Karen Wilkin

1. *Vie des Arts*, Vol. XX, Numéro 80, Automne 1975. Interview with Alfred Pellan, p.20.
"Le surréalisme vise à la création d'un monde poétique, illimité, jamais vu. Il faut inventer quelque chose, un monde différent."

2. André Breton, *Manifeste du Surréalisme*, Paris, 1924. Quoted by William S. Rubin, *Dada, Surrealism and their Heritage*, Museum of Modern Art, N.Y., 1968, p.83.

3. André Breton, quoted by Rubin, p.83.

4. Paul-Emile Borduas, "En Regard du Surréalisme Actuel", *Refus Global*, Montreal, 1948, reprinted in *Borduas et les Automatistes*, Musée d'art contemporain, Montréal, 1971, p.117.
"Les surréalistes nous ont révélé l'importance morale de l'acte non préconcu."

5. Paul-Emile Borduas "En Regard du Surréalisme Actuel", reprinted in *Borduas et les Automatistes*, p.117.
"Si j'ai la certitude d'etre devant un Mousseau, c'est à cause d'une relation plastique, fatale et constante à Mousseau que ma mémoire me rapelle comme une chose unique et propre à tous les objets qu'il façonne."

6. Robert Motherwell, interviewed by Max Kozloff, *Art Forum*, September 1965, p. 34.

Pierre Gauvreau   *Sans Titre*   oil on canvas   23½″x41½″   1947   Musée d'art contemporain, Montréal

Paul-Emile Borduas *Mes Pauvres Petits Soldats* oil on canvas 19″x22″ 1949 Flora Parlee

Jean-Paul Riopelle   *Le perroquet vert*   oil on canvas   43⅜″x55⅛″   1949   Le Musée de Québec

New Internationalism: Abstraction in Montreal and Toronto

Paul-Emile Borduas   *Expansion Rayonnante*
oil on canvas   45¾"x35"   1956
Dominion Gallery

Guido Molinari   *Tri-vert*   acrylic latex on canvas
40½"x67"   undated   Edmonton Art Gallery

Jock Macdonald
Primordial Fire
oil on board   53¾"x48"
1957
Agnes Etherington Art Centre

William Ronald *Slow Movement* oil on canvas 48″x95½″ 1953 Robert McLaughlin Gallery

John Meredith   *Painting #1*
oil on canvas   50"x42"   1962
Isaacs Gallery

Graham Coughtry
Two Figure Series XIX
oil on canvas   72″x60″
1964   Mr & Mrs Avrom Isaacs

Gordon Rayner   *River Window*
acrylic on canvas   70"x50"   1965
Barrie Hale

Jack Bush *School Tie*
oil on canvas 88½"x69" 1958
Robert McLaughlin Gallery

The perennial search for Canadian cultural identity has finally become a cliché, occupying an uneasy position somewhere between hockey as a national pastime and Mountie jokes as a national embarrassment. Happily, the pursuit of quality has taken precedence over the hunt for cultural identity for an impressive number of recent Canadian artists.

This is not to say that nationalism is a dead issue. Far from it, although both nationalist and "internationalist" Canadian artists of the past two decades are united by a common desire to be in the first rank, to be individual, to be current and significant. Yet this is self-evident. No serious artist, no matter how passionate his concern for Canadian "content", aspires to be minor or provincial. Difficulties arise because the centres of innovative, challenging art of the past have been outside of Canada. It is clearly impossible for a serious artist to ignore the achievements of the best of his colleagues, no matter what their nationality (a characteristic which separates the amateur from the professional) and this casts doubts on the claims of many Canadian nationalist artists that their work owes nothing to anyone — at least anyone outside of Canada. They insist they respond only to the special qualities of their environment and to The Canadian Experience. At the same time, their commitment to modernism (and therefore mainstream art of the recent past) is manifest in their work.

The issue is confused by one of the mysteries of modern Canadian thinking about the visual arts: abstract art is frequently New York-influenced, and is therefore held to be somehow non-Canadian. Figurative art, whether derived from California funk, New York pop, or American neo-realism, is hailed as indigenous grassroots expression as long as it contains overtly Canadian references — catch phrases, slogans, maple leaves, beavers, or hockey players.

Ironically, New York now houses a conspicuous number of representational artists who are as vocal in their rejection of New York abstraction as any Canadian populist, yet to date no one has accused Canadian figurative painters of following their example. Apparently one's mode of painting doesn't matter as long as what one paints is recognizably Canadian. This is less mysterious if we consider that abstract art, by its very nature, strives to be non-referential, non-specific, and is automatically removed from the literal allusions upon which grassroots evocations depend. The literal content of a painting of grazing elk is instantly recognizable and can outweigh the importance of formal derivation. The formal presence of bars of colour, in a painting made up of nothing else, is overwhelming. In the painting of elk, "what" can seem more important than "how", in spite of the fact that it is "how" rather than "what" which determines the success of the painting.

Canadian populists evidently fear that the special characteristics of Canadian-ness will be diluted if artists permit themselves to be influenced by how non-Canadians make art. Initially, this seems like nonsense; the history of art proves that both national and period styles are unavoidable and inevitable. Yet this fear is not wholly irrational (although it has as much to do with the proximity of New York and with economic and political issues as artistic ones). Because of Canada's peripheral position, the history of Canadian art is a history of responses to outside influences — and the imitation of mainstream styles by artists isolated from the mainstream could stand as a definition of provincialism. Yet, even if, as the populists claim, isolation can lead to invention, major art since about 1850 (and even before) has been about other art more than about self-expression. Serious artists who have chosen to separate themselves from metropolitan art-producing centres have still had to take into account the best work of those centres.

The development of abstract painting in Canada since the 1950s reflects these opposing views. It is a history of polarizations, of reactions and challenges: innovative art versus conservative art, *some* Canadian art versus *most* Canadian art, foreign art versus homegrown art. The fears of the populists have been justified by artists who aped the manner of mainstream art, without grappling with the issues which provoked it, but there are others who have successfully come to grips with the accomplishments of their predecessors and colleagues (wherever from) and made them the foundation of personal and original art. They are tied to place, but they have aspired to the best and in doing so they have shown us what first-rate Canadian art can be.

In turn, this high quality strengthens nationalism in the best way. The fact that Vittorio de Sica was an extraordinary filmmaker makes the world take Italian filmmaking seriously. The fact that de Sica was Italian or that his films were rooted in Italian experience is not the whole explanation of what made him an extraordinary filmmaker. The same could be said about Jack Bush and Canadian painting.

20th century European painting came late to Canada, but it came first to Montreal. Returned expatriates like Lyman and later, Pellan, made young Montreal artists aware of advanced European painting, while the Contemporary Art Society did a great deal to create a stimulating atmosphere, if admittedly for a small group. Although still isolated, Montreal in the 1940s saw the emergence of young, ambitious painters committed to modernism and to abstraction — the Automatistes and Prisme d'yeux. These movements were short-lived (a number of the Automatistes fled to France after World War II, while members of Prisme d'yeux changed aesthetic allegiance) but during the 1940s and early 1950s they set new standards for Montreal painters. By the 1950s, they were recognized and had received considerable acceptance.

The next generation was predisposed to abstraction, as much because of the Automatistes' example as developments in American painting, but they rejected the gestural paint handling and emotionally-charged imagery which characterized not only the Automatistes but most Abstract Expressionist painting of the period. In 1955, four of these young Montrealers united as "Les Plasticiens" — Louis Belzile, Jean-Paul Jérome, Fernand Toupin and "Jauran" (the critic Rodolphe de Repentigny). They were later joined by Fernand Leduc. In the approved Gallic manner, following the tradition of the Automatistes,

Prisme d'yeux, and innumerable European prototypes, they issued a manifesto of their beliefs. They declared themselves for pure, formal construction and for the elimination of the subjective, but admitted their indebtedness to the Automatistes.[1] Much of their aesthetic seems similar to Mondrian's statements in "Plastic Art and Pure Plastic Art", and, in fact, in an article in January 1955, de Repentigny cited Mondrian's painting as an example of "majestic purity and rigor",[2] praising it for its "elimination of all subjective trappings".[3]

The paintings of the Plasticiens are built of clearly-bounded geometric shapes, flatly and smoothly painted. The interlocking, jigsaw-like compositions owe something to Mondrian, something to Russian Constructivism, and a great deal to Synthetic Cubism — hardly radical styles in 1955. But whatever their merit or lack of it, the Plasticiens provided the possibility in Montreal of a different and more austere kind of painting than the stormy outpourings of the Automatistes.

The detached, theoretical content of the Plasticiens' Manifesto is a sign that significant changes had taken place in Montreal's art world since the Automatistes had issued *Refus global* less than a decade earlier. The Plasticiens spoke of painting and aesthetic problems; the Automatistes had addressed themselves almost equally to social and artistic questions. Yet another indicator of change was Guido Molinari's Galerie l'Actuelle, founded in 1955 as the first Montreal gallery dedicated exclusively to non-figurative art. Its existence bears witness to vigorous activity in Montreal at the time; the Automatistes' first exhibitions (with rare exception) had been held in improvised spaces and borrowed apartments. Despite Molinari's personal preference for the Plasticiens' ideas, the coexistence of Automatiste and Plasticien aesthetics was reflected in l'Actuelle's opening show, which included Borduas, Riopelle, Mousseau, Leduc, Molinari, Jean McEwen, Ulysse Comtois, Rita Letendre and Claude Tousignant.

The developed work of Molinari and Tousignant (and to an extent Letendre) continues the beliefs of the Plasticiens. Their paintings of the 1960s share a typically Montreal preoccupation with cool geometry, anonymous surfaces, and blazing colour treated as an optical phenomenon. Both Molinari and Tousignant reduced composition to restatements of the shape of the canvas (or perhaps vice versa). The equilibrium of this simple geometry is destroyed by dazzling juxtapositions of raw colour. Yves Gaucher's less chromatic abstractions of the period similarly depend on optical effects.

Optical zap seems typical of Montreal painting even today, among painters as diverse as Letendre, Guy Montpetit, Jacques Hurtubise, Denis Juneau, and a number of younger painters. Often pictures all but disappear in a flux of visual sensation. There is also a coexisting strain of greyed-down colour in Montreal (often allied with pronounced texture): even Molinari and Gaucher have recently abandoned startling optical effects in favor of cooler colours which guarantee a more coherent surface. Curiously, although there frequently is a lot of very intense colour in Montreal painting of the 1960s, it rarely seems to be structural. Instead, colour appears to have been applied to a preconceived image; it does not seem to be what determined that image.

The industrial brilliance of acrylic paint is offered as an antidote to severely intellectualized structure and anonymous surfaces. Molinari, Gaucher, and Tousignant all work in series, often altering nothing but the size of the canvas or the direction of divisions. Even though the painter doesn't know how a sixteen-foot grey, green, and yellow painting will differ in effect from the eight-foot version until he has actually made it, the pictures are largely preconceived. The Automatiste practice of letting the painting evolve as the result of a series of (ostensibly) unwilled decisions has been totally discarded in favor of systems and equations. Sometimes the place a painting occupies within a system or series appears more important than what it looks like.

Several Montreal painters have remained apart from either Automatiste-derived expressionism or Plasticien-sanctioned geometry. John Fox, who is somewhat removed from the Montreal establishment by his Anglophone status, has pursued a personal brand of all-over lyrical painting. Jean McEwen has continued to make luminous, hieratic images with richly-worked leathery or ceramic-like surfaces. McEwen and Fox have looked away from Montreal — Olitski and Rothko come to mind immediately as antecedents — but at the same time they belong to the European-oriented tradition of Montreal modernism. They are related to artists like Toupin and Jacques de Tonnancour whose highly-textured tonal paintings are in turn derived from European contemporaries.

Charles Gagnon, who may be the most interesting painter in Quebec at the moment, is unique in appearing to have absorbed both the lessons of the Automatistes and those of the Cubists and Surrealists who influenced them. American Abstract Expressionism, particularly that of de Kooning and Johns, evidently held his attention, but Gagnon, who has spent a good deal of time in New York, freely admits his interest in New York painting. His paintings certainly are based on different premises than his Montreal contemporaries: Gagnon's spontaneity, generous handwriting, and odd colour sense set them apart. Although he leaves obvious clues to which painters have influenced him, Gagnon's paintings suggest an individual response to current ideas, rather than provincial imitation.

For all Montreal's reputation as a center of radical art in Canada, its abstract painters of the 1950s and 1960s often seem paradoxically conservative. For the most part, they appear to strive for anonymity, using carefully preconsidered structure, systems, impersonal surfaces, and colour, either unified by greyness or by nameable out-of-the-tube hues. The danger lies in paintings being so objectified, so rationalized that they become refinements which lend themselves to intellectual dissection, but fail to challenge preconceptions of what painting can be. They can become emblems of logic and good taste, neutral fields for contemplation. Charles Gagnon is distinguished by his apparent willingness to take risks in his paintings rather than trusting to predictable, known solutions or relying on intellectual formulae. In this, he seems closer to his Montreal predecessors of the 1940s than to his contemporaries.

A recent statement by Molinari could serve as evidence of the problem. He spoke of covering up sections of a picture as they were painted, so as not to know what he had done,[4] in order to free the next section from the influence of an earlier decision. The elimination of conscious decision-making is part of automatist practice, but given Molinari's history of opposition to the Automatistes, it suggests other motivations. His smooth surfaces and neutral geometry imply an attempt to get the artist's hand out of the picture. His publicized picture-making while blindfolded and in pure darkness[5] was a self-avowed effort to "destroy what (he) knew about painting".[6]

Philip Guston told a similar story in the early 1960s. To keep from using easy colour solutions, he forced himself to use different colours than those that first came to mind — red when he wanted to use blue, green when he thought of orange. The difference between Guston's and Molinari's methods is that Guston kept looking at the result, allowing what had already been painted to determine the painting's progress, retaining the power to accept or destroy what he had done. The analogy is perhaps a little too neat, but a good deal of Montreal painting of the 1960s suggests that super-cool intellectualism has prevented looking around.

In the 1940s, the Automatistes had addressed the problems posed by some of the most advanced painting of their time, continuing and advancing the cause of the French-speaking Canadian avant-garde. In the 1950s, the Painters Eleven in Toronto became the first English-speaking Canadians to deal with that challenge.

Toronto in the 1950s had no real tradition of adventurous painting, practically no connection with advanced European art. The Group of Seven and their heirs continued to dominate through the established exhibitions of the Ontario Society of Artists and the Royal Canadian Academy. The Art Gallery of Toronto reinforced this conservatism. The artists of Painters Eleven came together simply because they were having difficulty finding a place to show.

In 1953, William Ronald offered to organize an exhibition of abstract paintings, as adjuncts to settings of contemporary furniture, for Simpsons Department Store, where he worked. "Abstracts at Home" included work by seven painters — Ronald, Jack Bush, Oscar Cahen, Alexandra Luke, Kazuo Nakamura, Roy Mead, and Tom Hodgson. Despite the furniture, they liked the idea of showing together, and proposed future abstract exhibitions with more artists. (It was obviously impossible for the Toronto avant-garde to continue as a group of seven.) Jock MacDonald, Harold Town, Walter Yarwood, and Hortense Gordon were asked to join, bringing the number to eleven.

Bush was the only member of the Eleven with a dealer — Roberts Gallery — and arranged a group showing in February, 1954. Painters Eleven continued to exhibit as a group until they disbanded in 1960. In 1956, they showed in New York with "American Abstract Artists" at the Riverside Museum; Ronald moved to New York and later signed with the prestigious Kootz Gallery, but continued some association with his Toronto colleagues.

The Painters Eleven, all committed to abstraction and modernism, were a stimulating presence for younger Toronto artists such as Graham Coughtry, Dennis Burton, Joyce Wieland, Michael Snow, Gordon Rayner, and John Meredith. The Riverside Museum show attracted favorable attention and Ronald enjoyed an initial success in New York. Toronto painters began to submit works and have them accepted at large international shows and elsewhere in Canada. Clement Greenberg paid a memorable visit in 1957, provoked by what he had seen in New York. All of this forced Toronto painters to take themselves seriously and expanded their ambition.

Barrie Hale, in his introduction to Toronto Painting: 1953-1965, describes the period as one of great energy and activity, when many galleries opened and artists became a far more conspicuous part of the life of the city. Toronto's expanded urban aspirations, including the greatly enlarged cultural life of the 1970s, date from this period. Hale characterizes both Bush's generation and the younger painters as sharing "aggressiveness ... a determination to get art out there in front of the public, not show one polite canvas a year at a Society show".[7] Aggressiveness, oddness, and lack of politeness were characteristic of Toronto painting of the 1950s and 1960s (and still are). The Toronto "look" is very different from the Montreal "look" of the same period. Toronto paintings are eccentric, full of quirky drawing and strange expressive colour; they are not objects like their Montreal counterparts.

Possibly because they had so little direct experience of Cubism, Surrealism, and advanced European art in general, Toronto painters were forced to more or less re-invent the history of modern art for themselves, which may account for the roughness and outrageousness of the best of Toronto painting. At first they were similarly isolated from advanced art of their own time; Jack Bush often spoke of the excitement which attended the first reproductions of contemporary art which reached Toronto in popular magazines such as Life and Time. Later, of course, they went to New York to see for themselves, and it is not an overstatement to say that confrontation with the real thing provoked greater seriousness and often better painting.

Yet Toronto pictures are unlike New York pictures, just as they are unlike Montreal pictures. Most are oddly pictorial; even when they are most flat and most lay-out-like, they are surprisingly animate. Unlike Montreal's reductive geometry, or New York's insistence on the painting as object, Toronto pictures tend to look as though their components had been jammed together, forced into or against the canvas, not deduced from it. Often there are latent figure or landscape references. Figure imagery is fairly explicit in Coughtry and Burton's work; nature is alluded to in a more general way in Gershon Iskowitz's paintings; Jack Bush found visual stimulus in anything from his garden to neckties and wrapping paper, although these stimuli are completely transformed and disembodied.

The novelty of Toronto's outburst of energy in the late 1950s and 1960s, which Hale describes, must have obscured, to some extent, distinctions between artists. It is easier to sort things out at this distance. Some of the second generation of Toronto modernists, such as Snow and Wieland, have abandoned "straight" painting for other media and other concerns. One can only speculate as to how their painting might have developed — Wieland was a lyrical and provocative painter in the early 1960s — if nationalism and pop imagery hadn't taken precedence. From the perspective of the mid-seventies, it is relatively easy to identify those who had mastered the manner but not the substance of 1950s abstraction and were unable to sustain the promise of their early work. Some have relaxed the vigor of early paintings in favor of popular images of Modern Art. Others, like Meredith, continue to hold our interest, if chiefly for sheer zaniness, which has had a considerable influence on Toronto's newest generation of painters. Jack Bush towers over most of his contemporaries, having left a stunning legacy — nearly twenty years of steadily growing achievement. Bush's independence of mind is part of his Toronto inheritance, as is his freedom from Cubist habits of composition. But the fact that he painted only for himself, supporting his family as a commercial artist, allowed him to preserve that independence. The paintings did not have to please anyone.

Bush's most important legacy to Toronto's younger painters — apart from his renowned courtesy and encouragement to young artists — may have been his extraordinary sense of colour. Most of Bush's generation and the next — the Meredith-Rayner generation — used colour for expression, not as a structural element. Violent light and dark contrasts, and brilliant Post-Impressionist chroma often seem more related to Tom Thomson than anything else. Many of the new generation of Toronto painters use colour as structure, to determine and build their

paintings. Although few achieve Bush's subtlety or richness of colour, they rarely sink to arbitrariness. Toronto's present population of younger artists have also inherited a new tradition of wackiness and eccentric personality from their predecessors. Their painting refuses to be ingratiating or to acknowledge conventional ideas of good taste — sometimes with brilliant results, sometimes disastrous.

But, in the best new artists, this independent spirit is based on the same deep affection and understanding of older masters — like Matisse — which informed Bush's work. Most of this generation has travelled more widely and probably seen more art than any of the Painters Eleven had at equivalent stages; yet most of them state that seeing paintings by Toronto artists when they were growing up was important to them. David Bolduc probably is typical of this generation: he still lives in the part of Toronto where he was raised, and the examples of Meredith and Rayner are clear in his work. He insists on the influence Toronto painters have had on him, but his awareness of international twentieth-century art is equally obvious. And he has said that it was a Matisse exhibition in Paris that made him want to be a painter.

The current generation of Canadian artists is scattered across the country, not tied exclusively to Montreal or Toronto. An observer of recent Canadian history and culture remarks that there is no single dominant centre, as there is in the United States. As a result, it seems more than ever possible for good art to be made anywhere in Canada. The Maritimes and the West Coast boast activity and enthusiasm, while a surprising number of gifted artists have chosen to work on the Prairies. William Perehudoff, Otto Rogers, and Ernest Lindner, to name only three, all elect to live in Saskatoon and continue to produce pictures which hold their own with any of their contemporaries. Of the large urban centres, Toronto seems particularly full of energy and full of young artists worth keeping an eye on, but it is not unique.

The bugbear of provincialism — of superficial imitation of major styles — still looms. One theory holds that the only guarantee of being in the mainstream is literal connectedness to the centres of mainstream culture, but old conditions for making art may not apply so strictly to present-day Canada. Western artists who feel no need to move east, for example, are proof. It takes more effort for artists in isolated areas to keep up with what their colleagues are doing and to visit important collections and exhibitions, but they make that effort.

Travel is relatively easy, if expensive, and despite the vagaries of weather and airlines, takes much less time than it did twenty years ago. Canadians are beginning to see more important art outside the major cities, thanks to travelling exhibitions, newly "decentralized" museums, local galleries, and private collectors. Malraux's "museum without walls" is a reality, although the dissemination of reproductions has had negative effects as well. (Anyone who has visited an art school in a remote area has come across students making pictures based on art magazine information.) The large urban centers are still important, yet new conditions in Canada make it possible for artists to survive and sometimes flourish in smaller cities, at surprising distances from traditional centres. The ubiquitous, indispensable Canada Council and some provincial government programmes have played a considerable role in establishing these new conditions. Perhaps they will create whatever will ultimately distinguish contemporary Canadian art.

Robert Motherwell claims that what was particularly American about American painting of the 1940s and 1950s was its violence.[8] Contemporary Canadian art is non-violent (for the most part) but full of energy: Barrie Hale's word "aggressive" seems apt. The most interesting Canadian artists are directing that aggression toward making the best art possible — what Jack Bush called "knocking the ball out of the park".[9]

Karen Wilkin

1. Manifesto issued 10 February 1955, *Manifeste des Plasticiens*, reprinted in exhibition catalogue *Jauran et les premiers Plasticiens*, Museé d'art contemporain, Montréal, 1977, unpaged.

2. "...l'exemple d'une pureté et d'une rigueur majestueuse..." Reprinted in *Jauran et les premiers Plasticiens*.

3. "...l'élimination de toute mise en scène subjective..." Reprinted in *Jauran* catalogue.

4. Statement made by Molinari at a Painter's Symposium at the Agnes Etherington Art Center, Queen's University, Kingston, Ontario. From panel discussion and public forum "Canadian Painting, 1977: Dead or Alive", March 3, 1977. Transcript published by Agnes Etherington Art Center, p. 46.

5. Transcript, p.32.

6. Transcript, p.32.

7. Exhibition catalogue *Toronto Painting: 1953-1965*. Ottawa: The National Gallery of Canada, 1972, introduction by Barrie Hale, p. 16.

8. Robert Motherwell, interviewed by Max Kozloff, *Art Forum*, September 1965, p. 34.

9. Jack Bush "Reminiscences". reprinted in catalogue of *Jack Bush: A Retrospective*, Toronto, Art Gallery of Ontario, 1976, unpaged, from a taped interview in the archives of the Robert McLaughlin Gallery, Oshawa.

*"I once told Mrs. Bundy
about staying in a village
where there seemed to be
nothing to paint. Laid out
on a flat plain, its one street
was so wide that I could not
get both sides in a
composition. It was hot;
the colour was all bleached
out of the sky; and it was
a case of trying to make
something out of nothing.
I walked around the town and
viewed it from all directions.
About three miles away I
found a cemetery; there was
not a tree, a flower, or even
a blade of grass. "Bury me
not on the lone prairie,"
I thought, as I turned away.
The village was not only
bleak, it had no character
at all. I could do nothing with
the place; it needed a chinook
or a cloudburst to liven it up."* [1]

A. Y. Jackson

Western Canada and the Emma Lake Workshops

In the 1940s and early 1950s, western Canadian art was dominated by Calgary. Walter Phillips and Illingworth Kerr were Post-Impressionists of the Group of Seven variety. Kerr had studied in the late 1920s at the Ontario College of Art. Phillips made Japanese and Art Nouveau-influenced woodcuts. The Banff School of Fine Arts, 80 miles away, attracted summer students from across the country. A. Y. Jackson taught summer classes there between 1943 and 1949.

The most radical modernists in the West during the 1940s and 1950s were William Leroy Stevenson and Maxwell Bates: the two artists had become convinced Post-Impressionists following a trip to the Chicago Art Institute in 1929. Bates moved to London, England in 1931, and didn't return to Canada until 1946. His mature style, heavily influenced by Max Beckmann, came about after studying with that artist and Abraham Rattner at the Brooklyn Museum Art School in 1949-50. W. L. Stevenson, an outspoken man, was a largely self-taught artist who admired French painting and French-influenced Canadian painters like Goodridge Roberts (although there is no evidence that he met or communicated with Roberts or any members of the Contemporary Art Society). His mature work, in an expressionistic, painterly manner reminiscent of Soutine, is still under-estimated.

Calgary's domination of the West waned in the 1950s, when a vital new art scene began to develop in the province of Saskatchewan. Following World War II, Saskatchewan emerged from a period of oversettlement followed hard upon by a devastating, depopulating drought which coincided with the economic depression of the 1930s. Perhaps stimulated by the "progressive", social orientation of the first socialist provincial government in Canada, its citizens sought to improve their cultural facilities. The nucleus of The Norman Mackenzie Art Gallery at Regina College in Regina was completed in 1953 and added to in 1958. Kenneth Lochhead was appointed head of the School of Art at Regina College in 1952. In 1956, he persuaded the University of Saskatchewan in Saskatoon to allow the summer art school facilities at Emma Lake in northern Saskatchewan to be used for an artists' workshop. In 1959, several other Regina artists, led by Ronald Bloore, the recently appointed director of The Norman Mackenzie Art Gallery, invited the American abstract painter, Barnett Newman, to lead an Emma Lake Workshop. Newman wasn't the first American workshop leader, but he was the first original, influential painter to lead one. The "Newman Workshop" brought together the nucleus of the Regina Five: R. L. Bloore, Art McKay, Douglas Morton and Ted Godwin (Lochhead, the fifth member, was in Italy on sabbatical leave in 1959; the sixth member, Roy Kiyooka, departed for Vancouver before the "Five Painters from Regina" exhibition, which Richard Simmins organized for The National Gallery of Canada in 1961). It also established the precedent of inviting artists with substantial international reputations to lead workshops throughout the 1960s.

The Canadian art world expanded enormously during the 1960s: public galleries multiplied; modernist art proliferated and became aligned with the contemporary international avant-garde for the first time in Canadian history. There were several reasons for this, among them the prosperity of the 1960s, the emergence of an outward-looking, post-war generation of Canadian artists, and the enormous influence of the new Canada Council, which helped Canadian artists establish contacts with the international art world. But probably the main reason was the sheer proximity of New York City which, following World War II, had become the centre of the international art world.

But if international influences spread across the nation, they seemed uniquely concentrated in Saskatchewan. The explanation for this was held to be a combination of provincialism and Emma Lake. Clement Greenberg, who led the 1962 Workshop, and artists associated with him, who also led Workshops, particularly Kenneth Noland (1963), Jules Olitski (1964), and Michael Steiner (1969), seemed to have had an extraordinary influence. But the very fact that these were only four of the workshop leaders during the decade suggests a more fundamental explanation.

By the late 1950s, Saskatchewan artists wanted to shake off the sense of being colonially dependent within Canada. If artists in Toronto and Montreal could relate directly to New York, so might they. And when they did, they chose the aspect of New York which seemed least provincial. In their eyes, this was abstract painting. Moreover, it was the kind of abstract painting which concerned itself least with "content", with "literature". Perhaps they felt literature entailed the regionalism and populism which had, in the past, led to provincialism and colonial dependence. In choosing to be influenced by advanced, abstract art, they accepted the possibility of succumbing to another kind of provincialism. They knew their art would inevitably reflect that of an avant-garde which worked under different social conditions in a powerful, international metropolis. But they felt that the alternative was even more debilitating. Realizing the risk it entailed, not the least of which was the certainty of being severely criticized in their own country, they chose to attempt to contribute to art rather than to Canadianism.

Modernist painting's rejection of "literature" favours a form of expression more closely aligned with the conditions of its own medium. This medium, it maintains, has its own story to tell and its own language to tell it in. But this "pure" painting has always been accompanied by parodies of itself. And these parodies invariably revert to a kind of "literature": they call up explanations and interpretations and dissertations on what modern art "means". They have tended to be avant-gardish movements like Dadaism, Surrealism, and, nowadays, varieties of Conceptual art. Occasionally they've been nationalist movements. Frequently they've been combinations of the two. But they're all obsessed with "meaning". They all subscribe to the notion that "form" in art is a kind of "delivery system" for "content".

In their opinion, this content must be recognizable apart from, or in relation to, the medium itself. They don't believe that expressiveness (i.e., content) can or should be embodied in, and subsumed by, the medium. The problem which arises when this implicit "formal" content conflicts with explicit information doesn't concern them. But forms and conventions speak in art. When they're taken for granted, all too often they speak against inspiration. The danger in adopting forms and conventions to tell a specific story lies in their tendency to tell a different, and often contradictory, story of their own. The artists in Canada who opposed nationalism and populism in art believed that real content came from working directly with the meanings and allusions embedded in forms and conventions themselves.

But the "literary" symbol style died hard. Even in Saskatchewan, it had its adherents. The first artists to emerge in Regina had a notion of content in painting which may have been held over from the Group of Seven and their followers. They painted like latter-day Symbolists — or proto-Symbolists. Only their symbolism derived from Surrealism and modern psychology rather than the "forms" of nature. Their art was based on the conviction that the proper subjects for abstract art should be drawn from the inner world of the psyche rather than the external, phenomenal world, and that these could be revealed by abstract symbols or signs.

In the hands of Bloore and McKay, this approach received its most intense development. Bloore, in 1958, painted a series of diamond-format paintings in which scraped cells of enamel paint spread across the entire surface of masonite panels, transforming the Cubist grid into a flat, all over configuration. Subsequently, he began to work in white-on-white impasto, creating simple cross and disc shapes, mostly with linear elements radiating from a centre. He felt these motifs were neutral and could be interpreted as the viewer chose. At best, the works have a reserved power.

The scraped enamel discs and rectangles McKay painted after 1961 were more consciously (or subconsciously) symbolic. But Bloore's own enamel paintings of the late 1950s lay behind them, as did Cubism and the all-over painting of Jackson Pollock (whose art McKay admired enormously). Whether McKay's images were or were not symbols of psychological states isn't provable. Certainly he seldom meant them to embody specific meanings. But their simple formats gave them a "presence" which invited conjecture. And they remain some of the best paintings produced in Canada during the decade.

The 1962 Emma Lake workshop led by Clement Greenberg provided the impetus for a new kind of Saskatchewan painting. The early workshops had been oriented toward New York and the international, modernist art world of the late 1950s. The second generation Saskatchewan artists weren't less concerned with content in their paintings, but they were less inclined to worry about the nature of it. Greenberg has been accused of establishing a formula for painting in western Canada, of turning Saskatchewan painters into slavish imitators of a particular New York style. Certainly Saskatchewan painters were New York oriented (and influenced) prior to his arrival. Some of them changed as a result of contact with him, just as Emily Carr changed after working with Mark Tobey, and some of those produced what Clement Greenberg called "Post Painterly Abstraction" (and what came to be known, more popularly, as "Colour Field Painting"). Their paintings contained relatively large expanses of saturated, soaked-in colour laid out in diagrammatic zones and areas. This sheer, phenomenal colour seemed too immediate, too actual, too "merely" decorative to contain content. As a result, the art of painters like William Perehudoff and Kenneth Lochhead was frequently criticized for being "empty". Some artists, notably Otto Rogers of Saskatoon, appropriated the colour washes from Colour Field painting to motifs — stylized trees and landscapes — which

suggested symbolism and content and, above all, a reference apart from the medium itself. Others, Dorothy Knowles in particular, returned to landscape painting, but to a variety of landscape painting which owed little to either the Group of Seven or the Contemporary Art Society (although Ms. Knowles admires the work of artists in both groups). This kind of landscape painting seemed to ignore meaning — especially symbolism — in favour of sheer immediacy. In favour, again, of "pure" painting.

If the early 1960s represented a great turn towards internationalism in Canadian art — a lowering of the barriers which had been erected by the Group of Seven — as the decade progressed, disillusion set in. The fact that the centre of the art world had shifted to North America, and to a city that was more accessible to most Canadians than to a vast number of Americans, was darkened by America's deteriorating international image, her deepening involvement in Vietnam, and the racism and violence which threatened her cities. American draft evaders sought refuge in Canada. American influence over the Canadian economy and Canadian politics was felt, increasingly, to be an unwarranted intrusion. The fear of U.S. expansion and "continentalism" was resurrected. Canadian artists began to worry, again, about a truly "Canadian" art.

Their concern had two consequences: they attacked the art and institutions which seemed to be influenced by the American art world and they promoted a new regionalism to counter the internationalism of avant-garde, abstract art. But once again, the critics of the "internationalism" (now "Americanism") were, themselves, modernists. And again, modernists attacked modernists over the issue of a national art. Only the new nationalists (with the possible exception of the Ontario-based ones)[2] were dedicated to some form of regionalism or populism, no great surprise in a vast, naturally-divided country.

Colour Field painting, in particular, was singled out for attack, just as Post-Impressionism in Montreal had been during the 1930s. It was regarded as a foreign import, an alien product with little or no relation to Canadian experience. Greenberg's relation to the artists whose work he championed was pointed to and deplored. His personal relation to the art world became an issue which tended to obscure his ideas as well as the nature of his influence. This hadn't happened in the 1930s with the influence of Roger Fry and Clive Bell. But Fry and Bell didn't visit Montreal, and didn't meet and personally influence Montreal painters. The very fact that they weren't French and had relatively little direct contact with the major artists of the School of Paris, much as they admired their work, made their opinions less inflammatory. Still, Greenberg's influence was not the real issue, any more than "Europe" had been during 1930s. The real issue was the fact that a foreign, "formal" art, with an apparent disregard for content, once again seemed to threaten an art which purported to be uniquely Canadian.

The fact that Colour Field painting did not claim a kind of content which could be separated from immediate, pictorial experience made it easy to attack on the grounds that it didn't apply itself to local, regional or national issues. In the mid and late 1960s, the more "literary" manifestations of the international avant-garde, those tracing their origin to Dada and Marcel Duchamp, were appropriated increasingly by Canadian artists with national and regional preoccupations. Like Post-Impressionist design, with its ability to accommodate symbols and thus proclaim "content", these other manners could deal with issues of one kind or another. Even — perhaps especially — when they failed to assimilate them into works of art, these issues could be recognized, interpreted, and discussed in ways which made even failed and feeble art seem justifiable.

Terry Fenton

1. A.Y. Jackson, *A Painter's Country*. (Toronto: Clarke, Irwin & Company, 1958), pp. 147-148.

2. Ontario had, and still has, the greatest stake in confederation. Natives of Ontario are the quintessential Canadians. Unlike the natives of other regions of Canada, they make no — or very little — distinction between their regional identity and their nationality. The fact that most of the nationalist movement in Canadian art (as opposed to regional, populist movements) have originated in that province suggests this.

W.L. Stevenson   *Autumn Bushes*   oil on masonite   10″x12″   undated   Edmonton Art Gallery

Maxwell Bates   *Landscape*   oil on masonite   23½″x30″   undated   Glenbow-Alberta Institute

Kenneth Lochhead
Red Contact
acrylic on canvas
79½″x67½″ 1964
Canada Council Art Bank

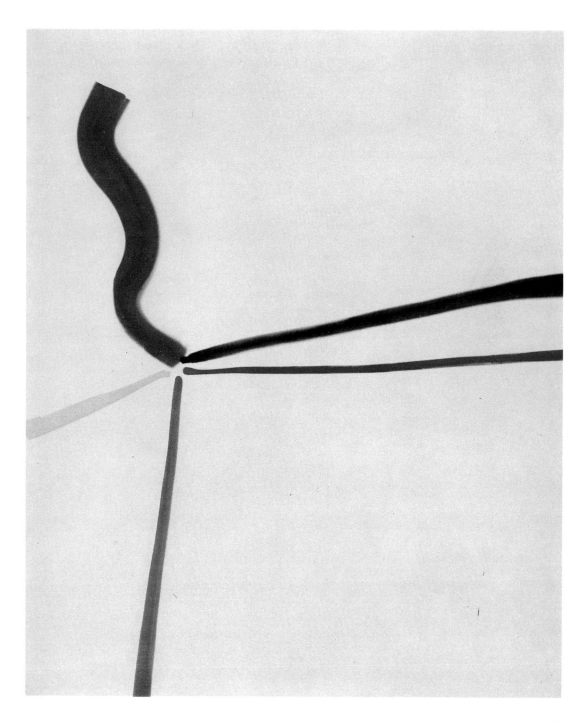

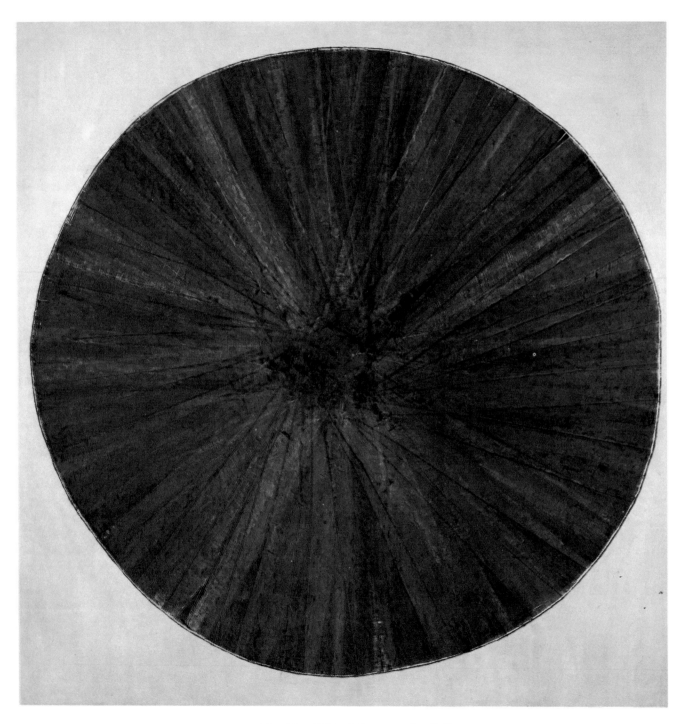

Art McKay   *Flux*   enamel on masonite   48"x48"   1964   Edmonton Art Gallery

Otto Rogers   *Sunset Stillness*   oil on canvas   60"x60"   1967   Saskatoon Gallery & Conservatory Corporation

Dorothy Knowles   *Summer Day*   acrylic on canvas   56″x72¾″   1969   Edmonton Art Gallery

William Perehudoff *Nanai #10* acrylic on canvas 78"x60" 1970 Rebecca Perehudoff

Regionalism, Populism, Anti-Americanism

Claude Breeze   *Grass, Sky, Trees, #2*
acrylic on canvas   178"x117"   1966
Canada Council Art Bank

Jean Paul Lemieux   *L'été*   oil on canvas   23x49¾″   1959   London Public Library & Art Museum

Joyce Wieland   *Time Machine*   oil on canvas   45"x45"   1960   Isaacs Gallery

Alex Colville   *Family and Rainstorm*   tempera on board   22½″x29½″   1955   National Gallery of Canada

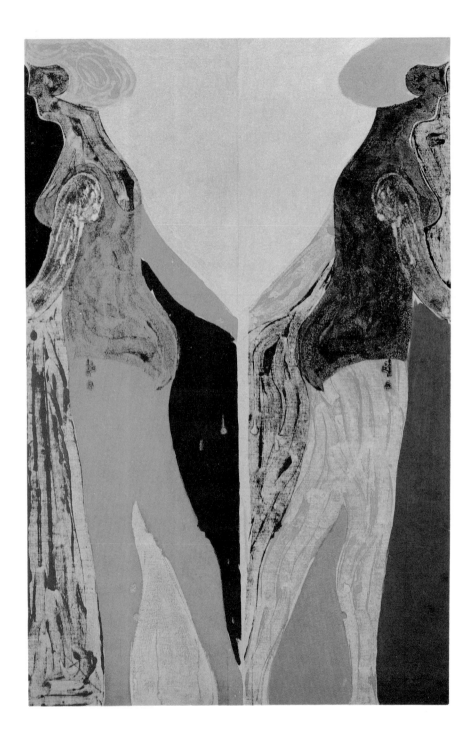

Michael Snow *Beach-hcaeb* oil on canvas
80"x50" 1963 University of Western Ontario

Greg Curnoe *For Ben Bella* mixed media
61¾"x49½"x38¾" 1964
Edmonton Art Gallery

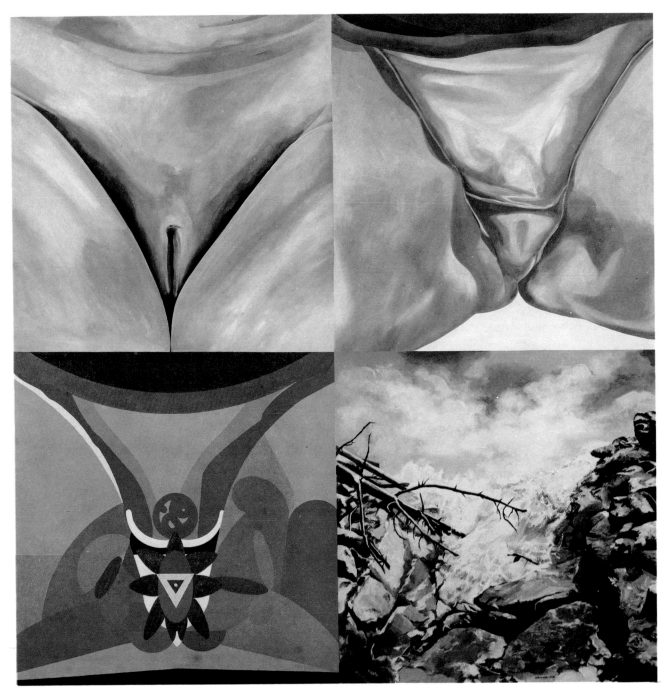

Dennis Burton   *Metamorphosis*   oil on canvas   60"x60"   1968   Isaacs Gallery

Regionalist, populist art isn't new in North America. The American Scene movement in the 1930s was basically a populist movement which reacted to and rejected contemporary French modernism — supposedly because it was French. Artists like Grant Wood, Thomas Hart Benton and Edward Hopper placed stylized figures in settings which conformed to clear, simple, Post-Impressionist design. But the American Scene wasn't the American landscape, let alone a wilderness landscape. It was a kind of social genre which depicted the American people, particularly farmers and workers. A "pure", Matisse-influenced landscape painter like Milton Avery didn't belong. His subjects — he preferred seagulls and sunbathers to workers — weren't "serious".

Populism in Canadian art didn't begin in the mid-sixties. It had antecedents. But these antecedents seldom influenced subsequent development — especially outside their regions.

Populist art, by its nature, doesn't seek an international audience. It's a regional art which, at the most, seeks national recognition. Although the Group of Seven was primarily an Ontario regional movement which spoke to all of Canada, it wasn't a populist one in the narrow sense. Its concern with establishing a Canadian identity didn't extend to depicting the Canadian people. Populist art almost invariably involves painting the figure. When it departs from the figure, it usually turns to the depiction of cultural settings. It prefers the hand of man to the hand of God.

If populism in Canadian art grew in strength in the late 1960s in the context of contemporary modernism, it had American Scene-style antecedents in Jean Paul Lemieux and Alex Colville. Lemieux and Colville are two of the finest artists to emerge in Canada since World War II. Colville has been influential in his native Maritimes and is largely responsible for the leaning toward what used to be called "magic realism" in that area. Lemieux has magic of his own, but seems to have had little influence on painters in his native Quebec — who have been influenced by various kinds of international modernism — despite his great popularity.

Lemieux is a French Canadian of the Contemporary Art Society's generation whose work is, if anything, flatter, more Cubist-influenced, more "abstract" than theirs. But his Cubist geometry contains specific, regional content which wasn't present in the art of the Contemporary Art Society. His figures are distilled and stylized from Quebec life. In the hands of a lesser painter, this could have produced a mawkish combination of abstraction and "content". But even when Lemieux gravitates towards sentimentality (especially when he depicts button-eyed children), he compensates by austere placement and judicious colour. At best, he's a refined painter who creates an intimate, provincial world peopled by flat, magical figures.

Two-dimensional design haunts Alex Colville's art, too. His full, modelled figures tend to be placed in settings which have been fitted into two-dimensional schemes. Colville has been compared to the American Andrew Wyeth. The comparison is only superficially apt. Local colour and nostalgic description count for far less in Colville's art; colour and a kind of simplified modelling count for much more. Like Lemieux, his figures have a frozen, monumental presence, and his pictures are governed by a stillness, reminiscent of Piero della Francesca, which is not characteristic of Wyeth. While Colville isn't a flat colourist like Lemieux, he uses strong, graphic design as a framework for a sense of light which bathes volume and space in a mysterious ambiance. This makes him — despite his provincial associations — less of a populist. Colville is more generalized and universal and less specifically Canadian than Wyeth is American.

Although Lemieux's and Colville's populism is neither anti-international nor anti-American, much of the populist art which emerged in Canada in the late 1960s is. Like the American Scene painters, the new Canadian populists have protested the influx of international modernism. In opposition to it, yet under its spell, they have struggled to establish an art for and about the Canadian *people*. In Ontario, this movement includes Greg Curnoe, Joyce Wieland, Claude Breeze, and John Boyle; in the west, Don Proch, Joe Fafard, and Harry Savage. It's a movement which includes writers and film makers as well as painters and sculptors. Because it isn't clearly defined, it's easily confused with the avant-garde movements which have proliferated in the past decade.

Although it tries to combine illustration with modernist design, it's an attitude, not a style, let alone a formally-oriented one. The Canadian populists share the American Scene painters' tendency to depict the human figure in a social or cultural context, or to depict the context itself. Despite their heightened colour and Cubist-influenced interlocking compositions, Greg Curnoe's paintings depict figures and cultural settings. Joyce Wieland's paintings evolved from comic-book depictions of disasters to quilts with Canadian slogans. During the mid-sixties, Claude Breeze produced a series of lovers in a landscape which recalled some of the themes — but not the style — of Thomas Hart Benton.

This latter-day populism frequently leans towards the Symbolist, Dadaist, Surrealist tradition and avoids Cubism, Abstract Expressionism, and the so-called "formalist" movements. While it has adopted modernist design, it adheres to the movements which have applied content to the innovations of preceding "formal" modernists. In so doing, it provides another example of the on-going quarrel between advocates of form and content in modern art. Throughout this century, some artists have feared a growing retreat of content and meaning in advanced art. That their fears have not been borne out is beside the point. Expression, no matter how different, remains. But this fear has prompted the invention of "spiritual" theories to justify an involvement with an advanced art which has systematically abandoned literary conventions. Artists have turned equally to "the people" and "the nation" for this kind of justification.

If Nationalist art isn't necessarily superior, it hasn't been — especially in Canada — inferior. Where the anti-nationalists offer Milne, Borduas, Roberts, and Bush, the nationalists can counter with Jackson, Varley, Lismer, Carr, and perhaps, Colville. Even granting the fact that the latter are international artists in disguise, the contest seems inconclusive. Obviously nationalist artists have used modernist pictorial conventions. Equally obviously Canadian modernists — with the possible exception of Jack Bush — haven't altered or influenced the course of art.

The controversy between nationalists and inter-nationalists in the U.S. was resolved more conclusively, simply because some American artists since 1940 *have* changed the course of art. But, however important "leading the way" and "influencing the course of art" are as motivations for aspiring artists, they are not ends in themselves. If artists have a real purpose, it's to make the best art they can, because the best is simply better — for anyone and everyone. Artists are individuals. No matter how much they are shaped by history (or nationality, or geography), their individual achievements, in the long run, shape *it*. And shaping history means reshaping conventions.

So, at bottom, the disagreement between nationalists and internationalists is about how art should be made and judged. Some nationalists seem to believe that appreciation depends on a certain kind of regional or national content, that this content, because of its familiarity, acts like a language through which form can be appreciated — like one of Shakespeare's sonnets is appreciated through the English language. This is simply wrong. If it were right, we couldn't appreciate the art of other nations and other cultures. Nationalists more commonly maintain that original art must be made from unique experience and that regional and national experience is the most unique experience available. This is plausible. Experience must contribute to art, if only because perception, conception, and appreciation are forms of experience. So national and regional experience can, and perhaps inevitably must, contribute to the making of art. But art draws on more than just nationality. Among other things, it draws on the experience of visibility itself and the experience of other art. In aligning at least one aspect of their art with some form of national experience, Canadian nationalists often produced outstanding art. But when they maintained that only national or regional experience could produce original art, they were not only wrong, they were intolerant. And since intolerance is the enemy of free expression, they became opponents of originality.

But intolerance is all too often answered with intolerance. To maintain, as many formal modernists have, that national or regional experience is inherently inferior is equally intolerant and equally wrong.

The test of this argument is in its results. In the United States, as in France before it, it was won, decisively, by the internationalists. Great art came about when artists freely modified and extended conventions. The American Scene failed to match that achievement, not because it was too nationalistic, but because it failed to extend or revitalize the conventions which circumscribed its art. It is true — and cannot be emphasized enough — that this failure was only relative. After all, it did produce a Hopper, and it can be argued that Hopper is the equal of Avery, just as it can be argued that Jackson and Carr, in Canada, are the equals of Roberts and Borduas. But neither Hopper nor Avery, nor Roberts nor Borduas, could match Jackson Pollock or Morris Louis at their best.

National identities may or may not be good things in themselves. At the moment, they seem to be inevitable and will probably continue to be so as long as the nation state survives as the dominant political institution in the world. But the influence nationalism has exerted over art is more problematic. While its ability to determine public taste and patronage in Canada has been considerable, its lasting influence has been relatively insignificant. The fact that Canadian nationalist and populist art, as well as formal modernist art, has invariably been influenced from abroad points to the fact that it is not indigenous. There is no Canadian *style*.

The battle between nationalism and internationalism fades when a country's art changes, or makes its mark on, the history of art. When it calls the attention of the world to itself, it becomes a national art. Then, when it supposedly demonstrates a national sense of form, it belongs most completely to the world.

No country has been able to maintain that achievement continuously. In relation to the history of art, Canada is a very young country and need hardly claim to have produced a great, indigenous art. But, nonetheless, it has achieved a great deal. Modern Art was planted in Canada in the early 20th century. Since that time it has consumed the creative energies of Canadian artists of all kinds. Their accomplishments have been substantial. They have brought art in Canada to the point where, today, it trembles on the threshold of more enduring achievement.

Terry Fenton

Biography of the Artists

Marcel Barbeau
1925-

Born, Montreal, Quebec. Shared studio with Riopelle; pupil of Paul-Emile Borduas at l'Ecole du Meuble, 1942. Was a part of the pictorial revolution against figurative art led by Borduas in Montreal and showed with the rest of the surrealist "Automatistes" painters. One of the most experimental of this group, he has exhibited in Montreal and New York. Presently lives in Chaville, France.

Maxwell Bates
1906-

Born in Calgary, Alberta. Mainly self-taught, studied art and architecture at the Provincial Institute of Technology and Art, Calgary, 1926-1927, under Lars Haukaness. Went to England to study architecture and painting on his own, 1931. Became a member of the "Twenties Group" in London. Served in British Army, 1940-1945. Lived in Calgary 1946-1962. Went to the United States where he studied with Max Beckmann and Abraham Rattner at the Brooklyn Art School, 1949-50. Wrote articles on the philosophy of art for such magazines as *Canadian Art* during the fifties. Designed St. Mary's Cathedral, Calgary, in partnership with A. W. Hodges, F.R.I.B.A. Member of the Canadian Group of Painters. Moved to Victoria, B.C., 1962, where he now lives.

Ronald Bloore
1925-

Born in Brampton, Ontario. Studied at the Department of Art and Archaeology, University of Toronto, 1949, and subsequently at the Institute of Fine Arts, New York University. Received his M.A. from Washington University, St. Louis, Missouri, 1953. Lectured in art at Washington University, 1953-1955. Studied in England (Courtauld Institute, University of London), Belgium and France, 1955-1957. Lectured at the University of Toronto, 1957-1958. Appointed Director of the Norman Mackenzie Art Gallery, Regina, 1958. Attended the Emma Lake Artists' Workshop under Barnett Newman, 1959. Received Canada Council grant to work on the Island of Lesbos, Greece, 1962. Began teaching at York University, Toronto, 1965. Paints austere relief-like paintings using enamel on masonite. Member of the "Regina Five". Lives in Toronto.

Paul-Emile Borduas
1905-1960

Born, St. Hilaire, Quebec. Learned about church decoration from Ozias Leduc, 1920-1931, with whom he decorated a number of Quebec churches. Studied at the Ecole des Beaux-arts, Montreal, 1923. Part-time professor of drawing at the Plateau School, 1927. Went to Paris in the same year to study under Maurice Denis and George Desvallières at L'Ecole des Arts Sacrés. Returned to Montreal, 1928, and taught drawing at the Collège André Grasset and Externat Classique St. Sulpice. In 1937 he succeeded Jean Paul Lemieux as Professor of Drawing, Decoration and Documentation for the Ecole du Meuble, Montreal where he taught Riopelle, Barbeau and Fauteux, 1943. Discovered the theories of automatism of the surrealist André Breton, 1938; became a founding member of the Contemporary Arts Society, 1939, which was finally split into the "Automatiste" group of painters under Borduas and the "Prisme-d'Yeux" group under Pellan. Moved to St. Hilaire, 1945; wrote his *Refus Global*, 1948, for which he was discharged from the Ecole du Meuble. Wrote *Projections Libérantes* 1949, describing the events resulting from his former publication. Moved to Provincetown, Mass. 1953, influenced by works of Franz Kline, de Kooning, Gottlieb, Motherwell and Pollock; moved to New York, 1954; travelled to Italy and Sicily, 1956; to Germany, Switzerland, Paris, Greece, Belgium, 1957-1959; exhibited in Montreal, Europe and New York. Died in Paris.

Claude Breeze
1938-

Born, Nelson, B.C. Moved to Saskatoon, Saskatchewan, where he studied under Ernest Lindner. Studied with Art McKay, Roy Kiyooka, Ronald Bloore and Ken Lochhead at the Regina School of Art, 1957-1959. Studied at the Vancouver School of Art, 1959-1960. Moved to North Surrey, a Vancouver suburb, 1969. Artist in residence, University of Western Ontario, London, 1972-1974; artist in residence at University of Calgary, fall, 1975. Visiting associate professor at York University, Toronto since 1976. Lives in North Surrey, B.C.

Dennis Burton
1933-

Born, Lethbridge, Alberta; studied drawing and graphics under Frederick Hagan and painting under Jock Macdonald at the Ontario College of Art, 1952; won a scholarship to the University of California where he studied under De Erdeley and Lebrun. Studied at the Skowhegan School of Painting in Maine, U.S.A. and has subsequently won numerous prizes, both for his painting and sculpture. Worked for C.B.C. until 1960 when he started painting full-time. Placing emphasis on content as well as style in painting, he is known for his "Garterbelt mania series." Lives in Toronto.

Jack Bush
1909-1977

Born in Toronto. Spent childhood in Montreal where he studied at the Royal Canadian Academy under Adam Sheriff Scott and Edmond Dyonnet, 1926-28. Studied at Ontario College of Art at night under Frederick Challener, John Alfsen, George Pepper, Charles Comfort and J. E. H. MacDonald, 1929-1939. Through publications and visits to New York and Montreal, he was influenced by the art movements in Paris and New York and learned about the ideas of John Lyman and of the "Automatistes". Showed with the "Painters Eleven" group of abstract artists in Toronto, 1953-1960; met Clement Greenberg in Toronto, 1957; resigned from all art societies, 1964; began painting in his own abstract style showing influences from the New York School and Matisse. Visited Europe and New York on Canada Council grant, 1962; visiting artist at Michigan State University, 1965; visiting artist, Cranbrook Academy of Art, Michigan, 1968. Retired from work as a commercial artist in 1968. Died in Toronto.

Emily Carr
1871-1945

Born, Victoria, B.C. Attended San Francisco School of Art, 1888; painted and taught in Victoria, 1895. Went to England and studied at the Westminster School of Art, London, c. 1899-1904, under Julius Olsson and John Whitely. Returned to Victoria, began to sketch Indian motifs, totem poles; visited Alaska. Painted on the northern coast of British Columbia each summer between 1905-1910. Studied at the Colarossi, Paris and under Harry Gibb at Cressy-en-Bri, Brittany, 1910-1912. Exhibited with Fauves and returned to Victoria, painting in a more Fauvist style.

Stopped painting for fifteen years until she was introduced to the Group of Seven. Made trips to eastern Canada, 1921-1940; returned east on several occasions as a contributor of the Group of Seven shows. Studied with Mark Tobey, 1928. Member of the Canadian Group of Painters, 1933. Painted extensively during the 1930s, turning her attentions to writing after 1937. Died in Victoria, B.C.

Alex Colville
1920-

Born in Toronto, Ontario. Moved to Amherst, Nova Scotia in 1929. Joined painting classes run by Mrs. Sarah S. Hart, woodcarver and painter, under the auspices of Mount Allison University. Studied Fine Arts at Mt. Allison University, Sackville, under Stanley Royle, 1938. Appointed war artist, 1944, and painted in the Mediterranean and North European areas. Returned to Mount Allison, 1946, as teacher of painting and drawing and art history, where he stayed until 1963, at which time he was able to support himself by painting. Member of the Canada Council Administration Board since 1966. Artist in Residence at West Berlin University, June-December, 1971. He now lives in Sackville, N.B., seldom making more than three or four of his "magic realist" paintings a year.

Stanley Cosgrove
1911-

Born in Montreal. Studied at the Ecole des Beaux-arts, Montreal under Henri Charpentier, Charles Maillard, and Joseph St. Charles, 1935-1937, and at the school of the Montreal Art Association under Edwin Holgate, 1938. Went to New York, 1939, then Mexico City where he studied fresco techniques under José Clemente Orozco, 1939-1943. Returned to Montreal, 1944, where he taught oil and fresco painting at the Ecole des Beaux-arts and was involved in textile design with Borduas, Maurice Raymond, Lapalme and Sullivan. Went to France, 1953, on Canadian government fellowship. Returned to continue teaching at the Ecole des Beaux-arts, Montreal. Member of the Canadian Group of Painters. Lives in Hudson Heights, Quebec.

Graham Coughtry
1931-

Born in St. Lambert, Quebec. Studied at the Montreal Museum of Fine Arts, 1948-1949, under de Tonnancour and Weber and at the Ontario College of Art, graduating in 1953. Visited Europe a number of times, 1951, 1953; worked in Ibiza, Spain, 1959-1961, 1964. Teaches at the Ontario College of Art. Lives in Toronto.

Greg Curnoe
1936-

Born in London, Ontario. Studied at H. B. Beal Technical School, London, 1954, under Herb Ariss and summer, 1956, at the Doon School of Art, Kitchener. Studied at the Ontario College of Art, 1957-1960. Returned to London, 1960; instrumental in founding *Region* magazine and the Nihilist Party, 1962, based on the Neo-Dada movement. Organized a "happening" in London, Ontario, called "The Celebration", 1962. A strong Canadian nationalist, he was a prime mover in the Canadian Artists' Representation. Wrote *Refus Continental* with John Boyle, repudiating continentalism in Canadian art. He is known for his lettrist, pop art. Lives in London, Ontario.

Lionel LeMoine FitzGerald
1890-1956

Born, Winnipeg, Manitoba. Studied at A. S. Keszthelyi's School of Art, Winnipeg, and was a full-time commercial artist by 1912. Attended the Art Students League, New York under Boardman Robinson and Kenneth Hayes Miller, 1921. Returned to teach at the Winnipeg Art School, 1924, and became principal in 1928. Became one of the last members of the Group of Seven, 1932, replacing J. E. H. MacDonald. Founding member of the Canadian Group of Painters, 1933. Visited and painted at Bowen Island, near Vancouver, during the summers of 1942, 1948, 1949. Visited Mexico, 1951. Died in Snowflake, Manitoba.

Charles Gagnon
1934-

Born in Montreal; studied graphic art and interior design at the Parsons School of Design, New York, 1956-1957, and painted under Paul Brach at the Art Students League, N.Y. 1956; influenced by composer John Cage, dancer Merce Cunningham and artist Robert Rauschenberg. Studied at New York University 1957 and at the New York School of Interior Design, 1957-1959. Returned to Montreal, 1960, where he presently lives. Has been a teacher in the Department of Visual Arts, University of Ottawa since 1975.

Yves Gaucher
1933-

Born in Montreal where he studied at the Ecole des Beaux-arts, specializing in printmaking, 1954-1960. Worked in prints until c. 1965 when he began painting abstract geometric canvases. Visited New York, 1962, where he saw the Rothko retrospective. Attended festivals of contemporary music in Paris, 1961-62, where he became familiar with twelve-tone and electronic music. Both experiences had an enormous influence on his painting. Lives in Montreal.

Pierre Gauvreau
1922-

Born in Montreal, enrolled in the Ecole des Beaux-arts, Montreal, 1937. Member of the Contemporary Arts Society, 1939. Served overseas in the Canadian Army during World War II. Returned to Montreal, c. 1940 and studied two more years at the Ecole des Beaux-arts. Exhibited with the "Automatistes" in 1946, 1947 and signed its manifesto, *Refus Global*, in 1948. Later he became involved in television, radio, film and theatre work, and began to exhibit his work again in 1961. Lives in Montreal.

Lawren S. Harris
1885-1970

Born, Brantford, Ontario. Studied at the University of Toronto and was taught drawing and painting in Berlin by Schlabitz, during which time he did sketching on a walking tour of the Austrian Tyrol, 1906-1907; visited France, Italy, England. Travelled to Palestine and Arabia with Norman Duncan as an illustrator for Duncan's "Going down to Jerusalem" published in *Harper's Magazine*, 1908-1909, and to Minnesota. Returned to Toronto 1910, where he became a member of the Arts and Letters Club of Toronto which became an important meeting place for the Group of Seven. Saw the Scandinavian artists' exhibition in Buffalo, 1913; painted landscapes of the "Ward" in Toronto, and in the Laurentians, the Ottawa River and Haliburton regions. In 1913, with Dr. James McCallum, he financed the Studio Building in which most of the Group of Seven painted at some time. Travelled and painted in Algoma, the Rockies and the Arctic, slowly developing an abstract style which matured in the late 1930s/early 1940s. Left Toronto, 1934; lived in New England, 1934-1939; Santa Fé, 1939-1941; settled in Vancouver, 1942. Member of the Group of Seven, 1920; founding member of the Canadian Group of Painters, 1933. Died in Vancouver.

Adrien Hébert
1890-1967

Born, Paris, France. Spent childhood in both Montreal and Paris; studied at Monument National, Montreal, 1904, under Joseph St. Charles, Edmond Dyonnet, Joseph Franchère, and Jobson Paradis. Studied under William Brymner at the Art Association of Montreal, 1907-1911. Studied painting of historical and archaeological subjects under Fernand Cormon, Paris, France, 1911-1914, and discovered works of French Impressionists. Returned to Montreal, 1914 where he was appointed Teacher of Drawing for the Montreal Academic Commission, a position he held for thirty-five years. Visited France frequently, elected member of the Royal Canadian Academy. Painted street scenes, docks, locomotives in Montreal. Died in Montreal.

Edwin Holgate
1892-1977

Born, Allandale, Ontario; entered the school of the Art Association of Montreal, c. 1904, studying drawing under William Brymner and Alberta Cleland. Studied at the Académie de la Grande Chaumière, Paris, 1912, under Claudio Castelucho and later under Lucien Simon and René Ménard. Served in the Canadian army in France during World War I, returning to Paris in 1920 to attend the Colarossi under Adolph Milman. Returned to Canada, 1922, where he opened a studio and taught wood engraving at the Ecole des Beaux-arts in Montreal, for six years. Accompanied Marius Barbeau and A. Y. Jackson to Skeena River, B.C., 1926, sketching totem poles. Member of the Beaver Hall Group in Montreal. Eighth member of the Group of Seven, 1931. Founding member of the Canadian Group of Painters, 1933. Official Canadian war artist with the R.C.A.F. during World War II. Worked in Montreal during the following thirty years, where he died.

Jack Humphrey
1901-1967

Born, St. John, New Brunswick. Studied at Mount Allison University. Studied under Philip Hale at the Museum of Fine Arts, Boston, 1920-1923 and under Charles Hawthorne at the National Academy of Design, New York, 1924-1929. Examined the work and theories of Hans Hofmann with two of his students, 1928. In 1930 studied drawing at the Académie de la Grande Chaumière, Paris; saw forty canvases of Cézanne, studied at the Hans Hofmann School, Munich, for two and a half months; visited Italy, Cologne, Holland, Belgium. Returned to St. John the same year. Visited Vancouver, 1933 and Mexico, 1938. Founding member of the Eastern Group of Painters, 1938 and the Contemporary Arts Society, 1939; received overseas fellowship in 1952 and spent thirteen months in Paris and two months in Britain. Returned to Canada and began painting in a purely abstract manner. Died in St. John.

Gershon Iskowitz
1921-

Born, Kielce, Poland. Studied at the Warsaw and Cracow Artist Academies, 1937, 1938; spent war imprisoned in Auschwitz and Buchenwald. Studied at Munich Academy of Fine Arts, 1945-1948, with Oscar Kokoschka. Came to Canada in 1949. Lives in Toronto.

Alexander Young Jackson
1882-1974

Born, Montreal; studied at the Monument National, Montreal, until 1905, at the Chicago Art Institute under Clute and Richardson, 1905-1907, and at the Académie Julian, Paris, under Jean Paul Laurens, 1907-1910. Travelled extensively throughout Europe; Italy 1910, 1912, France 1910, 1911 and England (Leeds) 1912, painting in the Late Impressionist style, returning to Montreal between visits. Was persuaded by Lawren Harris and J. E. H. MacDonald to leave Montreal for Toronto, 1913. He worked in the Studio Building intermittently between 1914-1954. Travelled and painted throughout Canada including Georgian Bay, Algonquin Park, Algoma, Quebec, Alberta, Alaska and the Yukon; went to Europe as a war artist, 1914-1918; taught at Banff School of Fine Arts, 1943-1949, moved to Manotik, then Ottawa, 1954, and eventually to the McMichael Conservation estate in Kleinburg. Member of the Group of Seven, 1920; member of the Canadian Group of Painters, 1933. Died in Toronto.

Frank (Francis/Franz) Johnston
1888-1949

Born and died in Toronto. Studied evenings under Gustav Hahn, and at the Central Technical School under William Cruikshank and George Reid, 1905. In 1908 he worked as a commercial artist at the Grip Studios and then attended the Pennsylvania Academy, Philadelphia, studying under Phillip Hale and Daniel Garber, 1909; worked as a commercial artist in New York and subsequently returned to Toronto, 1915. In 1918 he received a commission from the Canadian War Memorials, for which he did seventy-three paintings. From 1918-1920 he joined MacDonald, Harris, Jackson and Carmichael on their trips to Algoma. Was a member of the Group of Seven from 1920-1922. Principal of Winnipeg School of Art, 1920-1924; in 1926 he started signing canvases Franz (rather than Frank) Johnston. Taught at the Ontario College of Art, 1927-1929; 1930-1940 established summer school of art at Georgian Bay. Travelled in Northern Ontario and the Arctic in thirties and forties.

Dorothy Knowles
1927-

Born in Unity, Saskatchewan. Received her B.A. from the University of Saskatchewan where she first studied painting under Eli Bornstein and N. Bjelejac, 1944-1948. Studied at the Goldsmith School of Art, London, 1951; travelled to France (Paris) and Italy with William Perehudoff, her husband, in 1952. Attended workshops at Emma Lake under such artists as Will Barnett, Joe Plaskett, Clement Greenberg, Kenneth Noland and Jules Olitski, 1957-1969. A landscape painter since 1962, she lives in Saskatoon, Saskatchewan.

Jean Paul Lemieux
1904-

Born in Quebec City where he spent his childhood. Met Parnell, an American muralist, and began to sketch on his own, 1914. Studied with the Brothers of the Christian Schools, Berkeley, California, 1916. Returned to Montreal, 1917. Enrolled in the Ecole des Beaux-arts, Montreal, 1926, studying under Charles Maillard, Edwin Holgate and Maurice Felix. Travelled to Europe, 1929, studying advertising art and following courses at the Académie de la Grande Chaumière and Colarossi, Paris; met Clarence Gagnon. Returned to Montreal, 1930, setting up a commercial art studio with Jean Palardy. Received diploma from the Ecole des Beaux-arts in 1934 and became a teacher with the school. Moved to Quebec City, 1937, where he taught at the Ecole des Beaux-arts. Went to France on a Canada Council Fellowship, 1954. During 1960s began to paint figures in landscapes. Retired from teaching in 1965. Now spends most of his time in Ile aux-Coudres, Quebec.

Ernest Lindner
1897-

Born, Vienna, Austria. Studied painting and drawing in school; went into the Austrian air force during World War I, then tried his hand at architecture, design, banking, business. Came to Canada in 1926 as farm labourer in Saskatchewan. Settled permanently in Saskatoon where he studied under Augustus Kenderdine, 1928. Did free-lance commercial art work and studied at the Technical College until 1935. Became art instructor and head of the Art Department at the Technical Collegiate, Saskatoon, 1936-1962. Canada Council grant took him to Europe where he travelled to England, France, the Netherlands, Germany, Italy, Switzerland and Austria; studied etching and wood sculpture at the Academy for Applied Arts, Vienna, 1959. Presently lives in Saskatoon.

Arthur Lismer
1885-1969

Born in Sheffield, England. Studied at the Sheffield School of Art, 1896-1906, and worked in Eadon Engraving Company and subsequently went to the Antwerp Academy 1906-1907; visited Paris, London, returned to Sheffield working as illustrator. Moved to Toronto in 1911 where he worked at the Grip Studios and then at Rouss and Mann, 1912. Principal of the Nova Scotia College of Art, 1916-1919, teacher at Ontario College of Art, 1919-1927; during this period he painted with Group of Seven in Algoma and the Rockies, but preferred to work in Georgian Bay area. Educational supervisor of the Art Gallery of Toronto, 1929-1936 where he introduced the theories of Viennese artist and teacher, Cizek. Invited to New Education Fellowship Conferences and travelled to France, England and South Africa, 1933; the United States, 1935, 1936; Australia and New Zealand, 1937. Lectured to art teachers in South Africa, 1936-1937; visiting professor at Teachers' College, Columbia University, spending time visiting New York, Iowa, Milwaukee, Massachusetts and New Jersey, 1938-1939; principal and teacher at the Montreal Museum of Fine Arts from 1940 on. Did much to encourage interest in both children and adults in the world of art appreciation. Member of the Group of Seven, 1920; member of the Canadian Group of Painters, 1933. Died in Montreal.

Kenneth C. Lochhead
1926-

Born in Ottawa. He studied at Queen's University, Kingston; Pennsylvania Academy, Philadelphia; and at the Barnes Foundation, Merion, Penn., 1945-1949. Appointed Director of the Regina College of Art, 1950. Involved in organizing the Emma Lake Artists' Workshops, 1955. Member of the "Regina Five". Visited Italy, summer, 1959. Included in the "Post Painterly Abstraction" exhibition in 1964 at the Los Angeles County Museum of Art. Taught in Winnipeg, 1964, and moved to Ottawa where he has taught at the University of Ottawa since 1975.

John Goodwin Lyman
1886-1967

Born, Biddeford, Maine, U.S.A. Spent childhood in Montreal. Studied at McGill University, 1905-1907; went to Paris, summer, 1907 and studied under Marcel Béronneau; in the fall he entered the Royal College of Art, South Kensington, London; studied at the Académie Julian, Paris, 1908, under Jean-Paul Laurens; met J. W. Morrice; joined Académie Matisse with English artist Matthew Smith, 1909; met Matisse a number of times; visited Pont Aven. Travelled through Switzerland, Normandy, Munich where he was impressed with the works of Goya and Cézanne. After a brief stay in Montreal 1911-1912, he returned to Paris; worked in the Red Cross during World War I; lived in Paris until 1931 during which time he travelled to Europe, North Africa, Bermuda, Los Angeles and Provincetown (where he met leading American painters, 1918). Returned to Montreal, established *The Atelier* in cooperation with Hazen Sise, George Holt, and André Bieler, 1931-1933; formed the Lyman Summer Art Class, St. Jovite; wrote art reviews for *The Montrealer*, 1936-1940; formed the Contemporary Arts Society and the Eastern Group of Painters, 1939. Associate Professor of the Department of Fine Arts, McGill University, 1948-1957, Chairman of the Department of Fine Arts, McGill University, 1957. Frequent trips made to Cape Cod and Barbados 1958-1960. Died in Barbados.

James E. H. MacDonald
1873-1932

Born, Durham, England; came to Canada in 1887. Studied at the Hamilton School of Art, 1887-1895, and at the Central Ontario School of Art and Design, Toronto, 1893-1895, under William Cruikshank and George Reid. Studied as an apprentice at the Toronto Lithographing Company during this time. Graphic designer at the Grip Studios, Toronto, 1895-1904, 1907-1911, and in London, England, 1904-1907. Began to paint seriously, 1912; saw exhibition of Scandinavian landscapes, Buffalo, 1913. Painted in Toronto, Georgian Bay, Thornhill (Ontario), the Laurentians, the Atlantic seaboard, the Rockies and Barbados, 1913-1932. Along with Lawren Harris, he was instrumental in bringing most of the Group of Seven together. Principal of the Ontario College of Art, 1928-1932. Member of the Group of Seven, 1920. Died in Toronto.

J. W. G. (Jock) Macdonald
1897-1960

Born in Thurso, Scotland. Studied at the Edinburgh College of Art until 1922. Fabric designer, 1922-1925, with Charles Paine; taught at the School of Art, Lincoln, England, as Head of Design, 1925. Moved to Vancouver, 1926, to become Head of Design at the Vancouver Art School. Sketched with Varley, 1927-1934. Became interested in twentieth century art (Kandinsky, Klee, Miro) after 1933. Formed the British Columbia College of Arts with Varley, 1933-1935. Lived in Nootka, B.C. 1935-1936. Returned to Vancouver and taught at the Canadian Institute of Associated Arts and at the Templeton Junior High School, 1938. Met Lawren Harris, 1944, and painted with him. Appointed Director of the Art Department of the Institute of Technology and Art in Calgary, 1942. Taught at the Banff School of Fine Arts, 1945, 1946. Appointed teacher at the Ontario College of Art, Toronto, from 1947-1960. Travelled to Europe on a Canadian Government Fellowship, 1954 (France, Scotland, England, Venice, where he met Chagall and Dubuffet), and to New York, 1956, to attend the American Abstract Artists show and William Ronald's show, 1957. Member of the "Painters Eleven", 1954-1960. Taught summers at the Doon School of Fine Arts, Kitchener, Ontario. Died in Toronto.

Jean McEwen
1923-

Born in Montreal. Studied pharmacy at the University of Montreal. Decided to become a painter c. 1949. Worked with Sam Francis, George Matthieu and Jean-Paul Riopelle in Paris, 1951-1953, and travelled to Brittany, Italy, Holland and Spain. Returned to Montreal and began to paint in an abstract manner. Member of Association des Artists Non-Figuratifs de Montreal; President, 1960. Visited New York, 1963. Lives in Montreal.

Art McKay
1926-

Born, Nipawin, Saskatchewan. Studied at the Provincial Institute of Technology and Art, Calgary, 1946-1948, where he came into contact with Jock Macdonald; and at the Académie de la Grande Chaumière, Paris 1949-1950; at the Columbia University, New York and the Barnes Foundation, Merion, Pennsylvania, 1956-1957. Began experimenting with non-objective art under the influence of the works of Pollock and his experiences with hallucinogenic drugs. Attended the Emma Lake Workshop under Barnett Newman in 1959. Member of the "Regina Five." Lives in Regina.

John Meredith (Smith)
1933-

Born in Fergus, Ontario, raised in Brampton; commuted to the Ontario College of Art, 1950-1953, studying under Carl Schaeffer, Eric Freifeld and Jock Macdonald; some influence by Borduas and the "Automatistes"; moved to Toronto, 1964, where he is presently living. Brother of William Ronald.

David Brown Milne
1882-1953

Born near Paisley, Ontario; studied under Frank V. Dumond and George Bridgman at the Art Students League, New York, 1903. Worked as a commercial artist in New York, met James Clarke who became Milne's patron, 1912. Attended French Impressionist exhibitions, witnessed the rebel exhibition of "The Eight", influenced by Maurice Prendergast. Included in Armory Show, N.Y., 1913. Enlisted in Canadian Army, 1918; was Canadian war artist in France and Belgium, 1919. Lived at Boston Corners, 1919. Taught in Ottawa and visited Montreal during 1923. Moved to Canada, 1928, staying at Lake Temagami during the summer, eventually living in a hut north of Georgian Bay, 1932-1939. Moved to Toronto, Uxbridge and Bancroft, Ontario. Died at Baptiste Lake, Ontario.

Guido Molinari
1933-

Born in Montreal; began formal art training at Ecole des Beaux-arts, Montreal, 1948-1950, and the School of Art and Design, Montreal Museum of Fine Arts under Marion Scott and Gordon Webber, 1951. Influenced at this time by the "Automatistes", Monet, Kandinsky, Russian Constructivists, the de Stijl Group and the Suprematists; c. 1954 became influenced by Mondrian. Began painting vertical colour stripe paintings in 1959. Member of "Les Plasticiens" group, 1954, and later of the Association des Artistes Non-Figuratifs de Montréal of which his Galerie L'Actuelle was the focal point. Taught at the School of Art and Design, Montreal Museum of Fine Arts, 1963-1965, and at Sir George Williams University. Lives in Montreal.

Jean-Paul Mousseau
1927-

Born in Montreal; studied at the Ecole du Meuble, Montreal under Frère Jerome, 1945-46; studied with Borduas, 1944-1951 and became a member of the "Automatistes", signing the *Refus Global* manifesto in 1948. Founding member of the Association des Artistes Non-Figuratifs de Montreal; member of the Société d'Art Contemporain, 1945-1950. Organized a "contre-salon", 1949, protesting against academicism at the Spring Salon in Paris. Works in a number of media (tapestries, ceramics, oils, stained glass). First artist in Montreal to integrate electricity into sculpture and painting. Has decorated a number of discotheques in Montreal and was commissioned to decorate one of the Montreal subway stations. Lives in Montreal.

Louis Muhlstock
1904-

Born, Narajow, Polland. Has lived in Montreal since 1911. Studied at the Monument National, 1918-1920 under Edmond Dyonnet and Joseph Saint-Charles; at the Art Association run by the Royal Canadian Academy under William Brymner, G. Horne Russell, Charles Simpson, Albert Robinson, Maurice Cullen, and Edmond Dyonnet, 1920-1926; and at the Ecole des Beaux-arts, Montreal under Charpentier, 1926-1928. Studied under Louis François Biloul in Paris, at the Académie de la Grande Chaumière, 1928-1931. Returned to Montreal, 1931. Member of the Contemporary Arts Society, 1939 and of the Canadian Group of Painters, 1942.

Toni Onley
1928-

Born in Douglas, Isle of Man. Came to Canada (Brantford, Ontario) in 1948, later moving to Vancouver. Studied at the Douglas School of Fine Arts; Doon School of Fine Arts, Kitchener, under Carl Schaefer; Instututo Allende, San Miguel d'Allende, Mexico, 1957-1959. Studied in England for a year on a Canada Council Grant, 1963. Presently working in Victoria, where he teaches at the University of British Columbia, Fine Arts Department. An abstract landscape painter, and print-maker.

Alfred Pellan
1906-

Born in Quebec City; studied at the Ecole des Beaux-arts, Quebec, 1920-1925. Went to Paris on a scholarship and stayed 15 years, 1926-1940, returning to Canada once, in 1936. Studied at L'Ecole Supérieur Nationale des Beaux-arts under Lucien Simon and at the Académie de la Grande Chaumière. Associated with artists such as Picasso, Miro, Léger and the Surrealists. Travelled to Greece, 1937. Returned to Canada, 1940, and became teacher of painting at Ecole des Beaux-arts, Montreal. Visited by Léger, 1945. Formed group of artists called "Prisme d'yeux," which counterbalanced the "Automatiste" movement of Borduas, 1948. Went to France, 1952-1955; returned to Montreal and worked on large commissions, set designs, costumes. Lives in Auteuil, Quebec.

William Perehudoff
1919-

Born in Langham, Saskatchewan. Studied at Colorado Springs Fine Art Centre under Jean Charlot, in New York at the Ozenfant School of Art and at the Carnegie Institute of Technology, Pittsburgh. Married Dorothy Knowles, 1951. Travelled and studied in England, France, Italy and America, 1952. Attended University of Saskatchewan's Emma Lake Artists' Workshops under Will Barnett, Herman Cherry, Clement Greenberg, Kenneth Noland and Donald Judd. Lives in Saskatoon.

Kenneth Peters
1939-

Born, Regina, Saskatchewan. Studied at the School of Art, Regina, Saskatchewan; attended Emma Lake workshops under Ferren, Greenberg, Olitski, Lawrence Alloway, and Frank Stella, 1962-1967.
He describes himself as an "organic colour painter." Moved to Montreal in 1969 where he presently lives.

Christopher Pratt
1935-

Born, St. John's, Newfoundland. Studied at The Prince of Wales College, St. John's, the Glasgow School of Art, and Mount Allison University, graduating with a B.F.A. in 1961. Having studied under Alex Colville at Mount Allison, Pratt's paintings have the same quality of still realism as his teacher's, but his austerity of line and his use of oil rather than acrylic make him stand apart from other realist painters. Pratt now lives in St. John's, Newfoundland.

Gordon Rayner
1935-

Born and lives in Toronto. Self-taught constructivist painter and sculptor; worked as a commercial artist at the age of sixteen, apprenticed to Jack Bush. Executed a large series of paintings done in the Magnetawan River District, Ontario, and travelled extensively throughout Europe, South America and the Middle East during the 1960s. Taught at the New School of Art, Toronto, 1968-1969; worked with Bob Rogers at the Nova Scotia College of Art and Design making prints, 1969.

Jean-Paul Riopelle
1923-

Born in Montreal. Studied as a child with Henri Bisson, a sculptor and painter, studied engineering at the Polytechnical Institute and took evening classes at the Ecole des Beaux-arts. Studied at the Ecole du Meuble under Paul-Emile Borduas, Marcel Parizeau and Maurice Gagnon, 1943. Became part of the nucleus of the "Automatistes" group; shared a studio with Marcel Barbeau and later with Jean-Paul Mousseau and Fernand Leduc. Has lived in France since 1946, making periodic visits to Montreal and, since 1974, to his studio at Lac Masson in the Laurentians. Works in many media.

Goodridge Roberts
1904-1974

Born in Barbados. Spent youth in Fredericton, New Brunswick; lived in London, England 1910-1912 and during World War I. Studied at the Ecole des Beaux-arts, Montreal, 1923. Studied under Boardman Robinson, John Sloan and Max Weber at the Art Students League, New York, 1926. Lived in Fredericton, painting watercolours, 1929. Lived in Ottawa, 1930. Artist-in-residence at Queen's University, Kingston, 1933-1936. Saw Morrice retrospective, Montreal, 1938. Opened school of art in Montreal with Ernst Neumann, 1936. Founding member of the Eastern Group of Painters and the Contemporary Arts Society, 1939. Canadian war artist in England, 1943-1945. Studied in France, 1953-1954. Artist-in-residence, University of New Brunswick, 1959. During 1950s and 1960s, he worked in Laurentians, Georgian Bay, Cape Breton Island, Eastern Townships and the Gatineau. Died in Montreal.

Otto Rogers
1935-

Born in Kerrobert, Saskatchewan. Studied art under Whynona Mulcaster, Saskatoon. Received a Masters Degree in Fine Art from the University of Wisconsin, 1959 and returned to Saskatchewan to instruct at the University of Saskatchewan, Saskatoon where he is now Head of the Art Department. He is both a painter and a sculptor. Worked and taught at Emma Lake, 1976 and 1977.

William Ronald (Smith)
1926-

Born, Stratford, Ontario. Studied at Ontario College of Art, 1947-1951, with Jock Macdonald and with Hans Hofmann, New York, 1952. Played a crucial role in the establishment of the "Painters Eleven", exhibiting with them in Toronto, 1953-1955, and New York, 1956. Left group to live in New York where he worked on contract for the Kootz Gallery until 1964 when he returned to Toronto and continued to paint and work as a broadcaster. Brother of John Meredith.

Jack Shadbolt
1909-

Born, Shoeburyness, England. Moved to Victoria, B.C., 1912. Travelled to Toronto, New York, Chicago and Detroit, 1933. Attended night classes at the Vancouver School of Art, 1934-1937, with Fred Varley. Studied in London with Victor Pasmore and in Paris with André Lhote, 1937. Taught at the Vancouver School of Art, 1938-1966, and at the Art Students League, New York, 1947-1948. Canadian war artist, 1944. Lectured at the Emma Lake Artists' Workshop, Saskatchewan, 1955. Visited France, Italy, Greece, 1957. A true West Coast artist, his stylized natural forms within an abstract framework show the influence of nature, oriental art and mysticism. Lives in Vancouver.

Jori Smith (Marjorie Thurston Smith)
1907-

Born in Montreal. Studied at the Ecole des Beaux-arts, Montreal, 1924-1929, at the School of the Art Association of Montreal under Randolph S. Hewton, and at the Council of Arts and Manufacturers under Joseph St. Charles and J. Y. Johnstone. Studied painting with Edwin Holgate, 1930. Travelled to England, France and Italy. Exhibited with the painters of the thirties and forties and then stopped painting entirely in the fifties, destroying most of her paintings. Went to Haiti in 1953; began showing again in the 1960s in Montreal. Lives in Senneville, Quebec.

Michael Snow
1929-

Born in Toronto; lived in Montreal, Toronto, Chicoutimi, and Winnipeg. Went to Upper Canada College. Studied at the Ontario College of Art, 1948-1949, graduating in Design. Musician and film-maker in the 1950s. Married Joyce Wieland in 1956. Developed the "Walking Woman" series in 1959. Moved to New York, 1963. Returned to Toronto 1971. Sculptor, video-artist and painter. Lives in Toronto.

William Leroy Stevenson
1905-1966

Born in Guelph, Ontario. Moved to Calgary at an early age. Primarily self-taught, he joined the Calgary Art Club, 1926. Attended drawing classes at the Alberta Institute of Technology, 1926-1927. Travelled to Chicago with Maxwell Bates to see Impressionist and Post-Impressionist works at the Art Institute, 1929. Moved to Vancouver with the C.P.R., 1946. Returned to Calgary, 1954, where he worked for the Calgary Allied Art Centre. Travelled to New York and Toronto in late 1950s. Taught at the Allied Art Centre, Calgary, and throughout Alberta. Died in an automobile accident in Clive, Alberta.

Philip Surrey
1910-

Born, Calgary, Alberta; studied at the Winnipeg School of Art, 1926-1927 under L. L. FitzGerald. Befriended F. H. Varley in Vancouver, and was influenced by his painting; studied three months with Frank Vincent Dumond and Alexander Abels at the Art Students League, New York, 1936; moved to Montreal, 1937, where he became photographic editor of the *Montreal Standard*. Influenced by Goodridge Roberts. Founding member of the Eastern Group of Painters and the Contemporary Arts Society, 1939. Travelled in Europe and the Orient. Lives in Montreal.

Tom Thomson
(1877-1917)

Born, Claremont, Ontario; spent his youth in Owen Sound. Commercial artist in Seattle, 1901-1905; at Grip Studios, Toronto, 1905-1912; and Rous and Mann, Toronto, 1912-1914, where he met most of the members of the future Group of Seven. Moved to the Studio Building, 1913, where he worked full-time. Painted during the summer with members of the Group in Algonquin Park, 1913-1917, making oil sketches which were turned into large, finished canvases in the winter. Although never an official member of the Group of Seven (he died before its formation in 1920), he inspired and was influenced by the new national-istic style of these artists. Died in canoe accident at Canoe Lake, Algonquin Park.

Claude Tousignant
1932-

Born in Montreal, studied at the Montreal Museum of Fine Arts, 1948-1952, under Arthur Lismer, Jacques de Tonnancour, Louis Archambault, Marion Scott and Gordon Webber; and at the Académie Ronson and the Académie de la Cloison d'Or, Paris, 1952; returned to Montreal, involved with the setting up of the Galerie L'Actuelle, 1956; member of the Association des Artistes Non-Figuratifs de Montreal. Lived in New York, 1964. Now lives in Montreal.

Harold Town
1924

Born in Toronto. Studied at Western Technical School, 1944 and at the Ontario College of Art in the late 1940s. Travelled to New York and Chicago where he gained familarity with the work of the Abstract Expressionists, 1948. Active member of the "Painters Eleven", 1953-1960, as both a painter and propagandist. Co-author of *Tom Thomson: The Silence and the Storm*. Lives in Toronto.

Frederick H. Varley
1881-1969

Born, Sheffield, England; studied at the Sheffield School
of Art and at the Antwerp Academy. Worked in London
as a commercial artist, 1904-1908, and in Sheffield,
1908-1911. Moved to Toronto, 1912, where he worked as
a commercial artist at the Grip Studios for three weeks
and then at Rous and Mann. Worked in Europe as a war
artist, 1914-1918. Painted at Georgian Bay; moved to
Vancouver where he was appointed Head of the Department of Painting and Drawing at the Vancouver School
of Art, 1926; painted a number of portraits; was influenced
by mysticism and oriental art; returned east to Ottawa,
Montreal and finally to the Toronto area. Member of the
Group of Seven, 1920; member of the Canadian Group
of Painters, 1933. Died, Unionville, Ontario.

Joyce Wieland
1931-

Born in Toronto. Studied at the Central Technical School,
Toronto under Carl Schaeffer, Doris McCarthy and
Bob Ross. Visited Europe in the 1950s. Returned to
Toronto. Married Michael Snow in 1956. Moved to
New York with Snow, 1963. Returned to Canada in 1971.
She is a painter, quilt-maker, film-maker and constructionist.
Lives in Toronto.

Selected Bibliography

Adamson, Jeremy.
Lawren S. Harris: Urban Scenes and Wilderness Landscapes 1906-1930,
exhibition catalogue. Toronto: Art Gallery of Ontario, 1978.

Borcoman, James.
Goodridge Roberts,
exhibition catalogue. Ottawa: The National Gallery of Canada, 1969.

Carr, Emily.
Growing Pains, The Autobiography of Emily Carr.
Toronto: Oxford University Press, 1946.

Duval, Paul.
Four Decades: The Canadian Group of Painters and their Contemporaries, 1930-1970.
Toronto: Clarke, Irwin & Co. Ltd., 1972.

Duval, Paul.
High Realism in Canada.
Toronto: Clarke, Irwin & Co. Ltd., 1974.

Fenton, Terry.
Jack Bush: A Retrospective,
exhibition catalogue. Toronto: Art Gallery of Ontario, 1976.

Fenton, Terry.
"Abstraction West: Emma Lake and After",
Journal, The National Gallery of Canada,
March 1976.

Groves, Naomi Jackson.
A. Y.'s Canada.
Toronto: Clarke, Irwin & Co. Ltd., 1968.

Hale, Barrie.
Toronto Painting: 1953-1965,
exhibition catalogue. Ottawa: The National Gallery of Canada, 1972.

Harper, J. Russell.
Painting in Canada.
Toronto: University of Toronto Press, second edition, 1977.

Hill, Charles C.
Canadian Painting in the Thirties.
Ottawa: The National Gallery of Canada, 1975.

Hubbard, R. H.
The Development of Canadian Art.
Ottawa: The National Gallery of Canada, 1963.

Hubbard, R. H.
Canadian Landscape Painting 1670-1930.
Madison: Elvehjem Art Centre, University of Wisconsin,
1973.

Jackson, A. Y.
A Painter's Country.
The Autobiography of A. Y. Jackson, Toronto:
Clarke, Irwin & Co. Ltd., 1976.

MacDonald, Colin S.
A Dictionary of Canadian Artists,
4 volumes. Ottawa: Canadian Paperbacks, 1967-1974.

McLeish, John A. B.
*September Gale, a Study of Arthur Lismer of the
Group of Seven.*
Toronto: J. M. Dent & Sons (Canada) Ltd., 1973.

Mellen, Peter.
The Group of Seven.
Toronto: McClelland and Stewart Ltd., 1970.

Murray, Joan.
The Art of Tom Thomson,
exhibition catalogue. Toronto: Art Gallery of Ontario, 1971.

Parent, Alain.
Jauran et les Plasticiens,
exhibition catalogue. Montréal: Musée d'art contemporain,
1977.

Pollock, Ann and Dennis Reid.
Jock Macdonald,
exhibition catalogue. Ottawa: The National Gallery
of Canada, 1969.

Reid, Dennis. *A Concise History of Canadian Painting.*
Toronto: Oxford University Press, 1973.

**Shadbolt, Doris, Karen Wilkin, Alvin Balkind,
Fernande Saint-Martin, and Allan MacKay.**
The Canadian Canvas,
exhibition catalogue. Toronto: Time Canada Ltd., 1975.

Silcox, David.
David Milne: 1882-1953,
exhibition catalogue. Kingston: The Agnes Etherington
Art Centre, 1967.

Silcox, David and Harold Town.
Tom Thomson: The Silence and the Storm.
Toronto: McClelland and Stewart, Ltd., 1977.

Teyssedre, Bernard and Fernand Dumond.
Borduas et les Automatistes 1942-1955,
exhibition catalogue. Montréal: Musée d'art contemporain,
1971.

Wilkin, Karen.
*The Collective Unconscious, American and Canadian Art:
1940-1950,*
exhibition catalogue. Edmonton: The Edmonton Art Gallery,
1975.

Wilkin, Karen and Roald Nasgaard.
Changing Visions,
exhibition catalogue. Edmonton: The Edmonton Art Gallery,
1976; Toronto: Art Gallery of Ontario, 1976.

Withrow, William.
Contemporary Canadian Painting.
Toronto: McClelland and Stewart Ltd, 1972.

The *Biography of the Artists*
and *Selected Bibliography*
have been compiled by
Elizabeth Brown.

About the Authors

Terry Fenton

Mr. Fenton was born in Regina, Saskatchewan and studied art and art history at Regina College and the University of Saskatchewan. In 1965, following three years in Edmonton working as a social worker, he was appointed Assistant to the Director of the Mackenzie Gallery in Regina.

In January of 1972, he was appointed Director of The Edmonton Art Gallery. Mr. Fenton has written extensively on contemporary art. In addition to organizing exhibitions relating to the history of art in western Canada, he has organized exhibitions of work by Larry Poons, Sidney Tillim, William Perehudoff and Michael Steiner. Recently he organized a retrospective of paintings by the late Jack Bush for the Art Gallery of Ontario.

Karen Wilkin

Ms. Wilkin was born in New York City and was educated at Barnard College and Columbia University. The recipient of a Fulbright Fellowship, she lived and studied in Rome between 1964 and 1965. She was Chief Curator at The Edmonton Art Gallery from July, 1971 to March, 1978. She has written and lectured extensively on Canadian and international contemporary art and is a recognized expert on the painting and sculpture of this century. Exhibitions she has organized include *Art in Alberta: Paul Kane to The Present, Sculpture in Steel, The Collective Unconscious, Tim Scott, Sculptures, The Fauve Heritage,* and *Adolph Gottlieb, Pictographs.* Ms. Wilkin presently works as a free-lance curator and critic in Toronto.